Contents

Introduction

This collection of four complete practice tests comprises papers from the *Cambridge English: First (FCE)* examination; students can practise these tests on their own or with the help of a teacher.

The *Cambridge English: First* examination is part of a suite of general English examinations produced by Cambridge English Language Assessment. This suite consists of five examinations that have similar characteristics but are designed for different levels of English language ability. Within the five levels, *Cambridge English: First* is at Level B2 in the Council of Europe's *Common European Framework of Reference for Languages: Learning, teaching, assessment*. It has also been accredited by Ofqual, the statutory regulatory authority in England, at Level 1 in the National Qualifications Framework. The *Cambridge English: First* examination is widely recognised in commerce and industry, and in individual university faculties and other educational institutions.

Examination	Council of Europe Framework Level	UK National Qualifications Framework Level
Cambridge English: Proficiency *Certificate of Proficiency in English (CPE)*	C2	3
Cambridge English: Advanced *Certificate in Advanced English (CAE)*	C1	2
Cambridge English: First *First Certificate in English (FCE)*	B2	1
Cambridge English: Preliminary *Preliminary English Test (PET)*	B1	Entry 3
Cambridge English: Key *Key English Test (KET)*	A2	Entry 2

Further information

The information contained in this practice book is designed to be an overview of the exam. For a full description of all of the above exams, including information about task types, testing focus and preparation, please see the relevant handbooks which can be obtained from Cambridge English Language Assessment at the address below or from the website at: www.CambridgeEnglish.org

Cambridge English Language Assessment
1 Hills Road
Cambridge CB1 2EU
United Kingdom

Telephone: +44 1223 553997
Fax: +44 1223 553621
email: helpdesk@cambridgeenglish.org

70082374

428.4
FCE/CAM

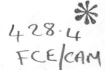

CAMBRIDGE
UNIVERSITY PRESS

Cambridge English

OFFICIAL
CAMBRIDGE
PREPARATION MATERIAL

FIRST 1

FIRST CERTIFICATE IN ENGLISH

WITH ANSWERS

AUTHENTIC EXAMINATION PAPERS FROM CAMBRIDGE ENGLISH LANGUAGE ASSESSMENT

CARDIFF AND VALE COLLEGE

For revised exam from 2015

Cambridge University Press
www.cambridge.org/elt

Cambridge English Language Assessment
www.cambridgeenglish.org

Information on this title: www.cambridge.org/9781107695917

© Cambridge University Press and UCLES 2014

It is normally necessary for written permission for copying to be obtained
in advance from a publisher. The sample answer sheets at the back of this
book are designed to be copied and distributed in class.
The normal requirements are waived here and it is not necessary to write to
Cambridge University Press for permission for an individual teacher to make copies
for use within his or her own classroom. Only those pages that carry the wording
'© UCLES 2014 Photocopiable' may be copied.

First published 2014
6th printing 2015

Printed in Italy by Rotolito Lombarda S.p.A.

A catalogue record for this publication is available from the British Library

ISBN 978-1-107-69591-7 Student's Book with answers
ISBN 978-1-107-66857-7 Student's Book without answers
ISBN 978-1-107-69448-4 Audio CDs (2)
ISBN 978-1-107-66331-2 Student's Book Pack (Student's Book with answers and Audio CDs (2))

The publishers have no responsibility for the persistence or accuracy
of URLs for external or third-party internet websites referred to in this publication,
and do not guarantee that any content on such websites is, or will remain,
accurate or appropriate. Information regarding prices, travel timetables, and other
factual information given in this work is correct at the time of first printing but
the publishers do not guarantee the accuracy of such information
thereafter.

The structure of *Cambridge English: First* – an overview

The *Cambridge English: First* examination consists of four papers.

Reading and Use of English   1 hour 15 minutes
This paper consists of **seven parts**, with 52 questions. For Parts 1 to 4, the test contains texts with accompanying grammar and vocabulary tasks, and separate items with a grammar and vocabulary focus. For Parts 5 to 7, the test contains a range of texts and accompanying reading comprehension tasks.

Writing   1 hour 20 minutes
This paper consists of **two parts** which carry equal marks. In Part 1, which is **compulsory**, candidates have to write an essay of between 140 and 190 words, giving their opinion in response to a task. In Part 2, there are three tasks from which candidates choose **one** to write about. The range of tasks from which questions may be drawn includes an article, an email/letter, a report and a review. In this part, candidates have to write between 140 and 190 words.

Listening   40 minutes (approximately)
This paper consists of **four parts**. Each part contains a recorded text or texts and some questions, including multiple-choice, sentence completion and multiple-matching questions. Each text is heard twice. There is a total of **30 questions**.

Speaking   14 minutes
This paper consists of **four parts**. The standard test format is two candidates and two examiners. One examiner takes part in the conversation while the other examiner listens. Both examiners give marks. Candidates will be given photographs and other visual and written material to look at and talk about. Sometimes candidates will talk with the other candidate, sometimes with the examiner, and sometimes with both.

Grading

The overall Cambridge English: First grade is based on the total score gained in all four papers. All candidates receive a Statement of Results which includes a profile of their performance in each of the four skills and Use of English. Certificates are given to candidates who pass the examination with grade A, B or C. Candidates who achieve grade A receive the Cambridge English: First certificate stating that they demonstrated ability at Level C1. Candidates whose performance is below Level B2, but falls within Level Bl, receive a Cambridge English certificate stating that they have demonstrated ability at Level B1. Candidates whose performance falls below Level Bl do not receive a certificate.

For further information on grading and results, go to the website (see page 4).

Test 1

READING AND USE OF ENGLISH (1 hour 15 minutes)

Part 1

For questions **1–8**, read the text below and decide which answer (**A**, **B**, **C** or **D**) best fits each gap. There is an example at the beginning (**0**).

Mark your answers **on the separate answer sheet**.

Example:

0 **A** have   **B** do   **C** get   **D** take

0	A	B	C	D
	▬	▭	▭	▭

Why we need to play

Human beings are not the only creatures that like to **(0)** ……….. fun. Many animals play, as do some birds. However, no other creatures spend so much time enjoying themselves as human beings do. Indeed, we **(1)** ……….. onto our sense of fun right into adulthood.

So why do human beings spend so much time playing? One reason is that we have time for leisure; animals have very little time to play as most of their life is spent sleeping and **(2)** ……….. food.

So, is play just an opportunity for us to **(3)** ……….. in enjoyable activities or does it have a more important **(4)** ……….. ? According to scientists, **(5)** ……….. from being fun, play has several very real **(6)** ……….. for us – it helps our physical, intellectual and social development. It also helps to **(7)** ……….. us for what we have not yet experienced. With very **(8)** ……….. risk, we can act out what we would do in unexpected, or even dangerous, situations.

1	**A** hold	**B** keep	**C** save	**D** stay
2	**A** searching	**B** looking	**C** seeking	**D** gaining
3	**A** engage	**B** combine	**C** contribute	**D** involve
4	**A** motive	**B** purpose	**C** intention	**D** cause
5	**A** excluding	**B** except	**C** apart	**D** away
6	**A** assets	**B** profits	**C** services	**D** benefits
7	**A** plan	**B** prepare	**C** practise	**D** provide
8	**A** brief	**B** short	**C** narrow	**D** little

Part 2

For questions **9–16**, read the text below and think of the word which best fits each gap. Use only **one** word in each gap. There is an example at the beginning (**0**).

Write your answers **IN CAPITAL LETTERS on the separate answer sheet**.

Example: | 0 | | B | E | E | N | | | | | | | | | | | | | | |

A bicycle you can fold up

Folding bicycles have (**0**) ……… around for quite some time now. However, an amazing new Japanese version (**9**) ……… be folded with a swiftness and efficiency never seen before. This bike is designed (**10**) ……… that it is possible to fold it up quickly. Once folded, you pull the bike along (**11**) ……… ease.

This remarkable bike has a half-folding frame with a hinge in the middle. And, although the basic idea is (**12**) ……… original, its inventor has created an especially clever variation, combining compactness (**13**) ……… convenience with smart design.

Recently, folding bicycles (**14**) ……… become very popular in Japan, particularly in congested urban areas like Tokyo, a city (**15**) ……… every square centimetre of space is in great demand. Japanese cyclists need to be able to store their bikes in tiny areas at home or the office. And (**16**) ……… they should want to take their bicycle on the underground, a folding model is a big advantage.

Part 3

For questions **17–24**, read the text below. Use the word given in capitals at the end of some of the lines to form a word that fits in the gap **in the same line**. There is an example at the beginning (**0**).

Write your answers **IN CAPITAL LETTERS on the separate answer sheet**.

Example:

0	E	X	T	R	E	M	E	L	Y									

Tea

Tea is an **(0)** ……..... popular drink with many people. It is estimated that   **EXTREME**

the consumption of tea in England alone exceeds 165 million cups daily.

Despite this, the drink was virtually **(17)** ……..... in England until about   **KNOW**

400 years ago. The first **(18)** ……..... to tea in England comes in a   **REFER**

diary written in 1660. However, its **(19)** ……..... really took off after the   **POPULAR**

(20) ……..... of King Charles II to Catherine of Braganza. It was her great   **MARRY**

love of tea that made it **(21)** ……...... .   **FASHION**

It was believed that tea was good for people as it seemed to be capable

of reviving the spirits and curing certain minor **(22)** ……..... . It has even   **ILL**

been suggested by some historians that it played a significant part in the

Industrial Revolution. Tea, they say, increased the number of hours that

(23) ……..... could work in factories as the caffeine in tea made them more   **LABOUR**

(24) ……..... and consequently able to work longer hours.   **ENERGY**

Part 4

For questions **25–30**, complete the second sentence so that it has a similar meaning to the first sentence, using the word given. **Do not change the word given.** You must use between **two** and **five** words, including the word given. Here is an example (**0**).

Example:

0   A very friendly taxi driver drove us into town.

DRIVEN

We .... a very friendly taxi driver.

The gap can be filled by the words 'were driven into town by', so you write:

Example:	**0**	*WERE DRIVEN INTO TOWN BY*

Write **only** the missing words **IN CAPITAL LETTERS on the separate answer sheet**.

---

25   They didn't sell many programmes at the match.

FEW

Very .... at the match last Saturday.

26   We got to work late because we decided to drive rather than take the train.

INSTEAD

We got to work late because we decided to drive .... the train.

27   Last Friday was the first time my car ever broke down, even though it is very old.

NEVER

Until last Friday, my car .... down, even though it is very old.

28 'All your complaints will be investigated by my staff tomorrow,' said the bank manager.

LOOK

The bank manager promised that his staff .... all our complaints the next day.

29 Last year the heavy rain caused the postponement of the tennis tournament.

BECAUSE

Last year the tennis tournament .... so heavily.

30 Jack does not want to work for his uncle any longer.

CARRY

John does not want .... for his uncle.

Part 5

You are going to read a magazine article about a famous pianist and the young student who became his pupil. For questions **31–36**, choose the answer (**A**, **B**, **C** or **D**) which you think fits best according to the text.

Mark your answers **on the separate answer sheet**.

A musician and his pupil

Paul Williams interviews the famous pianist Alfred Brendel.

Over six decades the pianist Alfred Brendel gradually built up and maintained a dominant position in the world of classical music. He was an intellectual, sometimes austere, figure who explored and recorded the mainstream European works for the piano. He wrote and played a great deal, but taught very little. Those who knew him best glimpsed a playful side to his character, but that was seldom on display in his concerts. It was a disciplined, never-ending cycle of study, travel and performance.

And then, four or five years ago, a young boy, Kit Armstrong, appeared backstage at one of Brendel's concerts and asked for lessons. Initially, Brendel didn't take the suggestion very seriously. He had had very few pupils and he saw no reason to start now. He quotes from another famous pianist: 'You don't employ a mountain guide to teach a child how to walk.' But there was something that struck him about the young boy – then about 14. He listened to him play. Brendel explained, 'He played remarkably well and by heart. Then he brought me a CD of a little recital he had given where he played so beautifully that I thought to myself, "I have to make time for him." It was a performance that really led you from the first to the last note. It's very rare to find any musician with this kind of overview and the necessary subtlety.'

As Brendel is bowing out of the public eye, so Kit is nudging his way into it – restrained by Brendel, ever nervous about the young man burning out early. Kit, now 19, is a restless, impatient presence away from the lessons – always learning new languages; taking himself off to study maths, writing computer code or playing tennis. All under the watchful eye of his ever-present mother. On top of all this he composes. 'This was very important,' Brendel says. 'If you want to learn to read music properly it is helped by the fact that you try to write something yourself. Then I noticed that Kit had a phenomenal memory and that he was a phenomenal sight reader. But more than this is his ability to listen to his own playing, his sensitivity to sound and his ability to listen to me when I try to explain something. He not only usually understands what I mean, but he can do it. And when I tell him one thing in a piece, he will do it everywhere in the piece where it comes in later.'

Brendel catches himself and looks at me severely. *line 50* 'Now I don't want to raise any expectations. I'm very cross if some newspapers try to do this. There was one article which named him as the future great pianist of the 21st century, I mean, really, it's the worst thing. One doesn't say that in a newspaper. And it has done a great deal of harm. As usual, with gifted young players, he can play certain things amazingly well, while others need more time and experience. It would be harmful if a critic was there expecting the greatest perfection.'

It is touching to see the mellowness of Brendel in his post-performing years. He explains 'When I was very young, I didn't have the urge to be famous in five years' time, but I had the idea I would like to have done certain things by the age of 50. And when I was 50, I thought that I had done most of those things, but there was still some leeway for more, so I went on. Although I do not have the physical power to play now, in my head, there are always things going on, all sorts of pieces that I've never played. I don't play now but it's a very nice new career.'

31 What is the writer emphasising in the first paragraph?

  A the wide range of music that Brendel has played
  B the total dedication of Brendel to his art
  C the reluctance of Brendel to take on pupils
  D the light-hearted nature of Brendel's character

32 Brendel uses the quotation about the mountain guide to illustrate that

  A it is not always easy to teach people the basics.
  B it is unwise to try to teach new skills before people are ready.
  C people can learn new skills without help from others.
  D it is unnecessary for an expert to teach people the basics.

33 What made Brendel first decide to accept Kit as a pupil?

  A He seemed so young and serious.
  B He was so determined and persistent.
  C He could play without the music.
  D He had an extraordinary talent.

34 Which of Kit's musical abilities does Brendel admire the most?

  A He is able to write music himself.
  B He is able to understand and respond to advice.
  C He can play a piece of music the first time he sees it.
  D He is able to remember all the music he has ever played.

35 Why does the writer use the phrase 'catches himself' in line 50?

  A He realises he has said too much to a journalist.
  B He doesn't enjoy giving interviews to journalists.
  C He wants to be careful he doesn't upset any music critics.
  D He resents the way that he has often been misquoted.

36 What is Brendel doing in the final paragraph?

  A justifying his lack of ambition when he was young
  B expressing regret at the loss of his physical strength
  C describing his present state of mind
  D explaining which pieces he prefers to play now

Part 6

You are going to read a newspaper article about a blind runner. Six sentences have been removed from the article. Choose from the sentences **A–G** the one which fits each gap (**37–42**). There is one extra sentence which you do not need to use.

Mark your answers **on the separate answer sheet**.

Blind Runner

Paul Hardy reports on a blind runner called Simon Wheatcroft who enjoys taking part in marathon and ultra-marathon races, running distances between 42 km and 160 km.

Running marathons, a race of 42 km, has become increasingly popular. This distance poses extreme physical and mental challenges for anyone, but for Simon Wheatcroft there is another hurdle; he has been blind since he was 18 years old.

For the past two years Simon, now 29, has been overcoming his disability to compete in marathons and ultra-marathons by training with runners who act as his guides, and also, rather uniquely, by teaching himself to run solo, out on the streets. 'I got bored exercising indoors, so thought, "I'll have a go at running outside",' he explains. **37** Then he got bored again and wanted to try running on the roads.

Weeks of gradual exploration followed, walking a route alone. **38** It took him along little-used pavements alongside a busy main road. He also recruited technology to help him form his mental map of the area using a smartphone app, to provide feedback through headphones about his pace and distance. This information could then be cross-referenced with his knowledge of the route and any obstacles.

Now, having covered hundreds of km alone on the route, Simon has been able, gradually, to phase out the app. 'When I first started I had to really concentrate to an unbelievable level to know where my feet were falling. Now it has become quite automated.' **39** 'I did make a few mistakes early on – like running into

posts. But you only run into a post once before you think "Right. I'm going to remember where that is next time",' he laughs.

Joining Simon for a training session, it's striking how natural and fluid his movement is; he takes shorter, shallower, more gentle steps than most runners, using his feet to feel his way. His landmarks are minute changes in gradient and slight variations in the running surface. **40** 'I have to believe this route is going to stay consistent, and there won't be things like roadwork signs or big rocks,' he says.

41 'I try to concentrate on the millions of footsteps that go right and think positively,' he explains. When it comes to racing in ultra-distance events, Simon has to use guides to run sections of the course with him; after all, it would be almost impossible to memorise a 150 km stretch of countryside by heart. However, the physical and practical advantages of training in the fresh air, on his own terms, are vast and have boosted his confidence in his running ability as well as providing inspiration to others.

But for Simon the real thrill and motivation for training come from simply being able to compete on equal terms. **42** 'I can't hide the fact I'm blind,' he says, 'but at the same time I would rather compete with everybody else and not be put into a special group. Being visually impaired doesn't mean you can't run.'

A These provide the familiarity and consistency essential for the blind runner.

B Their support gave him extra confidence regarding his changing surroundings.

C Simon believes the feelings of liberation and independence he gets from running solo far outweigh any anxiety over such dangers.

D He began by training on football pitches behind his house, running between the goalposts.

E It gives him a great opportunity to run with everyone.

F That's not to say the learning curve has been without incident.

G As a result of this slow experimentation, he was able to memorise a set five-kilometre course.

Part 7

You are going to read an article in which four graduates discuss going to university. For questions **43–52**, choose from the graduates (**A–D**). The graduates may be chosen more than once.

Mark your answers **on the separate answer sheet**.

Which graduate

says people should be allowed to consider a range of options apart from university?	**43**	
says that some people are expected to make important decisions before they are ready?	**44**	
initially rejected something she was told?	**45**	
was unaware of the alternatives to university?	**46**	
says that the type of learning at university is different from that at other institutions?	**47**	
felt when she was a student that she might not be doing the right course?	**48**	
says that some people discover that what is studied at university is not useful in the workplace?	**49**	
was uncertain about her reasons for going to university?	**50**	
says graduates have an advantage when applying for jobs?	**51**	
was expected to go to university despite being a fairly average student at school?	**52**	

Why go to university?

Four graduates talk about their experiences.

A Sonia

While I was doing my physics degree people would often say I was acquiring skills I'd be able to use in my future career, even if I didn't become a physicist. It sounded like nonsense to me: if I did another job in the end, what could be relevant about knowing what's inside an atom or how to operate a laser? It turns out they were referring to the wealth of other skills you pick up along the way. Communication and problem-solving are just two of these. In contrast to the way you may have been taught before, university teaches you to be innovative and to think for yourself. Going to university is about more than just studying though! I got to make friends from all over the world and they have proved to be useful work contacts.

B Jane

I went to university because it was the career path expected by school, parents and classmates (to an extent) and also because I didn't really have a clue about what other options were open to me. It's difficult to know how things would have turned out if I hadn't gone. I do know that the job I do 'requires' a degree to do it, though there must be alternative ways of developing these skills. The degree, like it or not, is the screening method used by large numbers of employers and as such opens certain doors. It's certainly harder to get into all sorts of careers without a degree. The debates about university education typically revolve around routes into employment, yet for many the degree is barely relevant to the work we end up doing later on. It gives access to a certain type of career but the actual degree can often be of little practical value.

C Lydia

There is a lot of pressure on teenagers to know exactly what they want to do with their lives. As a high-achieving student at school, the alternatives to university didn't really appeal to me. So I took up a place at a good university but ended up studying something I wasn't sure I was interested in. Some people know what they want to do from a young age, and for those people, going to university straight out of school may be a great idea. However, many of us are very unsure of our future ambitions aged 18, and should therefore be given as many choices as possible, rather than being pushed into a degree course. Many of my friends went to university straight from school.

D Bethany

I don't really remember making the decision to go to university. Everyone always assumed I would, even though I was never the most gifted academically. Someone asked me during my second year why I had gone, and I remember not being able to answer the question. Maybe it was the way I was raised? Maybe it was the school I went to? But university was the next step. I had a great time there, I must say. It's so much more than the place you go to get a degree. You learn so many life skills that I would urge anyone to give the idea some thought. Since graduation I've had a string of jobs. University is an excellent decision for some, and may provide the right qualifications to start a career. But for others, going straight into a job is just as appropriate.

WRITING (1 hour 20 minutes)

Part 1

You **must** answer this question. Write your answer in **140–190** words in an appropriate style on the separate answer sheet.

---

1   In your English class you have been talking about life in the past. Now, your English teacher has asked you to write an essay.

Write an essay using **all** the notes and give reasons for your point of view.

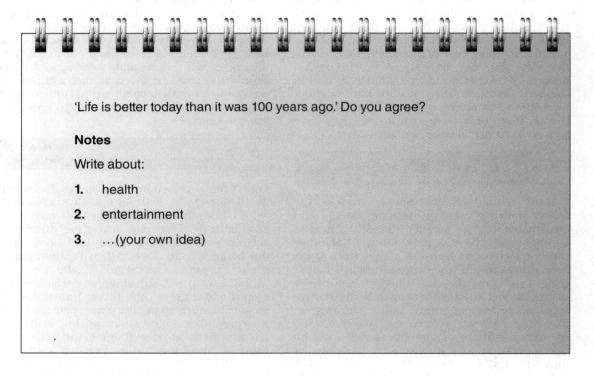

'Life is better today than it was 100 years ago.' Do you agree?

Notes

Write about:

1.   health

2.   entertainment

3.   …(your own idea)

Write your **essay**. You must use grammatically correct sentences with accurate spelling and punctuation in a style appropriate for the situation.

Part 2

Write an answer to **one** of the questions **2–4** in this part. Write your answer in **140–190** words in an appropriate style on the separate answer sheet. Put the question number in the box at the top of the answer sheet.

---

2   You recently saw this notice on an English-language website called TV Gold:

> **Reviews wanted!**
>
> ### A TV documentary I learnt a lot from.
>
> Have you seen an interesting TV documentary recently that you learnt a lot from? Write us a review of the documentary. You should explain what the documentary was about, tell us what you learnt from it and say whether other people would find it interesting too.
>
> The best reviews will be posted on the website next month.

Write your **review**.

3   You see this announcement on an English-language travel website.

> **ARTICLES WANTED**
>
> # A day in the city!
>
> We are looking for articles about how a visitor could have a great time in a city in your country in just one day.
>
> Write us an article telling us what a visitor can do, what they can see and how they can travel around.
>
> The best articles will be posted on our website.

Write your **article**.

4   Your English teacher has asked you to write a report on a part-time or holiday job that you have done. The report will appear in the college English-language magazine.

In your report, you should

- describe the job
- explain what you learnt from it
- say whether you would recommend other students to do it.

Write your **report**.

LISTENING (approximately 40 minutes)

Part 1

You will hear people talking in eight different situations. For questions **1–8**, choose the best answer (**A**, **B** or **C**).

1   You hear a woman talking on her mobile phone about a missing piece of furniture.
    How does she feel?

   A irritated with the removals company

   B unsure what's happened

   C anxious to find it quickly

2   You hear two students talking about their current course topic.
    What do they agree about?

   A how boring it is

   B how difficult it is

   C how relevant it is

3   You hear two business people talking about a contract.
    How does the man feel now?

   A frustrated because of the time wasted

   B surprised about the cancellation of the contract

   C sympathetic towards the other company's problems

4   You hear an artist telling a friend about an art prize he's just won.
    What is he doing?

   A expressing surprise

   B admitting that he's excited

   C explaining why he thinks he was chosen

5   You overhear a women talking to a friend on her mobile phone.
        Why is she phoning?

   A   to explain a delay

   B   to change some plans

   C   to make an arrangement

6   You hear a guitarist talking about his profession.
        What is the purpose of his talk?

   A   to warn about the challenges of becoming a musician

   B   to give step-by-step guidance on setting up a band

   C   to emphasise the importance of having loyal fans

7   You hear a woman talking to a sales assistant.
        Why can't she have a refund for her trainers?

   A   The receipt is wrong.

   B   She is not in the right shop.

   C   The trainers are no longer new.

8   You hear a woman talking about a radio chat show.
        What does she like about the show?

   A   The presenter makes her laugh.

   B   Information is given in an interesting way.

   C   Guests reveal quite a lot about themselves.

Part 2

You will hear a photographer called Ian Gerrard talking about his career. For questions **9–18**, complete the sentences with a word or short phrase.

Ian Gerrard – Photographer

The subject that Ian studied at university was [_____ **9**]

Ian did a presentation on [_____ **10**] as part of his final year.

Ian worked for a [_____ **11**] in the USA for a year after leaving

university.

When he travelled around the USA, Ian chose [_____ **12**] as the

theme for his photographs.

Ian says that [_____ **13**] is the season when he takes the

best photographs.

When Ian came back to Britain, he travelled around by [_____ **14**]

taking photographs.

Ian says he was surprised by how few photographers specialise in shots of

[_____ **15**] communities.

Ian's book will be available in bookshops in [_____ **16**] next year.

The title of Ian's book is [' _____ ' **17**]

Ian has chosen [_____ **18**] as the theme for his next tour.

Part 3

You will hear five short extracts in which people are talking about the benefits of learning another language. For questions **19–23**, choose which benefit (**A–H**) each speaker has experienced. Use the letters only once. There are three extra letters which you do not need to use.

A   It has boosted my intellectual abilities.

B   It has improved my chances in education.

Speaker 1 | 19

C   It has made me sensitive to global issues.

Speaker 2 | 20

D   It has allowed me to gain faster promotion.

Speaker 3 | 21

E   It has made getting around in other countries easier.

Speaker 4 | 22

F   It has allowed me to help other people.

Speaker 5 | 23

G   It has advanced my awareness of the way language works.

H   It has helped me make friends.

Part 4

You will hear an interview with a woman called Patricia Jones, who is a naturalist. For questions **24–30**, choose the best answer (**A**, **B** or **C**).

24 Looking back at her work, Patricia feels

    A surprised that her projects still attract volunteers.

    B proud of the wide influence she's had.

    C pleased by how she's regarded in Africa.

25 How does Patricia spend her time nowadays?

    A persuading people to alter their behaviour

    B advising governments on conservation

    C studying wildlife in its natural habitat

26 How does Patricia feel about zoos?

    A They all ought to be closed down.

    B They should have an educational purpose.

    C They still have a role to play in conservation.

27 In her new book, Patricia hopes to give

    A encouragement to young scientists.

    B advice on helping endangered animals.

    C guidance to other environmentalists.

28 Patricia believes that children should spend time in the natural world because

    A it is the only way to find out about it.

    B it is essential for their development.

    C it is a chance to change their view of animals.

29 The organisation called *In Touch* encourages young people to

    A be tolerant of each other.

    B actively work for change.

    C talk about their problems.

30 What does Patricia particularly want to do next?

    A to help girls who want to be scientists

    B to get scientists to be more responsible

    C to change people's attitudes to science

SPEAKING (14 minutes)

You take the Speaking test with another candidate (possibly two candidates), referred to here as your partner. There are two examiners. One will speak to you and your partner and the other will be listening. Both examiners will award marks.

Part 1 (2 minutes)

The examiner asks you and your partner questions about yourselves. You may be asked about things like 'your home town', 'your interests', 'your career plans', etc.

Part 2 (a one-minute 'long turn' for each candidate, plus a 30-second response from the second candidate)

The examiner gives you two photographs and asks you to talk about them for one minute. The examiner then asks your partner a question about your photographs and your partner responds briefly.

Then the examiner gives your partner two different photographs. Your partner talks about these photographs for one minute. This time the examiner asks you a question about your partner's photographs and you respond briefly.

Part 3 (4 minutes)

The examiner asks you and your partner to talk together. You may be asked to solve a problem or try to come to a decision about something. For example, you might be asked to decide the best way to use some rooms in a language school. The examiner gives you some text to help you but does not join in the conversation.

Part 4 (4 minutes)

The examiner asks some further questions, which leads to a more general discussion of what you have talked about in Part 3. You may comment on your partner's answers if you wish.

Test 2

READING AND USE OF ENGLISH (1 hour 15 minutes)

Part 1

For questions **1–8**, read the text below and decide which answer (**A**, **B**, **C** or **D**) best fits each gap. There is an example at the beginning (**0**).

Mark your answers **on the separate answer sheet**.

Example:

0   **A** predictable   **B** steady   **C** respectable   **D** main

0	A	B	C	D
	▬	▭	▭	▭

Home and abroad

After a short time living in a foreign country, I noticed conversations with locals assumed a **(0)** .... pattern. There were standard answers to the usual questions. Most questions caused little **(1)** .... – it was rather like dancing, where both partners know how to avoid **(2)** .... on each other's toes.

But, 'When are you going home?' was a question I **(3)** .... to answer, whenever I **(4)** .... my life and the direction it seemed to be **(5)** .... In the last ten years, I had lived in a dozen countries. And I had travelled through dozens more; usually in **(6)** .... of a purpose or a person; occasionally to see the attractions.

This kind of travel is not **(7)** .... wandering, but is the extensive exploration of a wide **(8)** .... of cultures. However, it doesn't allow you to put down roots. At the back of your mind, though, is the idea of home, the place you came from.

1	**A** puzzle	**B** trouble	**C** obstacle	**D** barrier
2	**A** touching	**B** moving	**C** walking	**D** stepping
3	**A** worked	**B** competed	**C** stretched	**D** struggled
4	**A** considered	**B** thought	**C** reflected	**D** believed
5	**A** making	**B** finding	**C** seeking	**D** taking
6	**A** look	**B** search	**C** sight	**D** inquiry
7	**A** aimless	**B** unreasonable	**C** unreliable	**D** indefinite
8	**A** difference	**B** arrangement	**C** variety	**D** order

Part 2

For questions **9–16**, read the text below and think of the word which best fits each gap. Use only **one** word in each gap. There is an example at the beginning (**0**).

Write your answers **IN CAPITAL LETTERS on the separate answer sheet**.

Example: | 0 | U | P | | | | | | | | | | | | | | | |

An Irish cookery school

In the last few years, a number of cookery schools have been set (**0**) ……... in Ireland to promote Irish cooking. (**9**) ……... such school is run by Kathleen Doyle not (**10**) ……... from the centre of Dublin.

'I opened the school twelve years ago,' says Kathleen. 'The school was by no means an overnight success; I found (**11**) ……... necessary to work hard to build up a reputation. One of my advantages was that I'd had problems with my own cooking. I've made (**12**) ……... mistake that it's possible to make, but (**13**) ……... of this, I know what people do wrong from first-hand experience.'

Just (**14**) ……... most cookery schools in Ireland, Kathleen initially copied the classical dishes of France and Italy and other countries (**15**) ……... have a reputation for excellent food. 'Now though, things are changing,' says Kathleen. 'We get excellent produce from Irish farms and, (**16**) ……... a result, we're encouraging students to create unique Irish dishes.'

Part 3

For questions **17–24**, read the text below. Use the word given in capitals at the end of some of the lines to form a word that fits in the gap **in the same line**. There is an example at the beginning (**0**).

Write your answers **IN CAPITAL LETTERS on the separate answer sheet**.

Example:

0	C	O	M	P	E	T	I	T	O	R	S							

Running speed

Elite (**0**) ..…..... like the Jamaican Usain Bolt have regularly been clocked **COMPETE**
running at nearly 45 kilometres per hour. Such speed would have seemed
(**17**) ..…..... not so long ago. Scientists now suggest that humans can **BELIEVE**
move (**18**) ..…..... faster than even that, perhaps as fast as 65 kilometres **CONSIDER**
per hour.

For years, it was assumed that simple muscle power determined human
speed, but recent research suggests otherwise. The most important
(**19**) ..…..... factor appears to be how quickly the muscles can contract **LIMIT**
and thus (**20**) ..…..... the time a runner's foot is in contact with the ground. **MINIMUM**

Is our athletic ability inherited? Researcher Alun Williams has (**21**) ..…..... **IDENTITY**
twenty-three inherited factors that influence sporting performance, such
as the (**22**) ..…..... use of oxygen, and strength. As world population rises, **EFFICIENCY**
predicts Williams, the (**23**) ..…..... of there being someone with the right **POSSIBLE**
genes for these twenty-three (**24**) ..…..... will increase noticeably and thus **CHARACTER**
faster runners are likely to emerge in future.

Part 4

For questions **25–30**, complete the second sentence so that it has a similar meaning to the first sentence, using the word given. **Do not change the word given.** You must use between **two** and **five** words, including the word given. Here is an example (**0**).

Example:

0 A very friendly taxi driver drove us into town.

DRIVEN

We .... a very friendly taxi driver.

The gap can be filled by the words 'were driven into town by', so you write:

| **Example:** | **0** | *WERE DRIVEN INTO TOWN BY* |

Write **only** the missing words **IN CAPITAL LETTERS on the separate answer sheet**.

---

25 Robert had never been to Turkey on business before.

FIRST

It .... Robert had ever been to Turkey on business.

26 It was impossible for me to know which road to follow.

NOT

I .... known which road to follow.

27 So far this year the cost of petrol has not increased.

INCREASE

So far this year there .... in the cost of petrol.

28   I cannot get all my clothes in the suitcase.

   BIG

   The suitcase .... take all my clothes.

29   The waiter carried the tray very carefully so that he wouldn't spill any of the drinks.

   AVOID

   The waiter carried the tray very carefully so .... any of the drinks.

30   I wasn't able to get to the airport on time because of the bad weather.

   PREVENTED

   The bad weather .... to the airport on time.

Part 5

You are going to read an article about an island off the west coast of Scotland. For questions **31–36**, choose the answer (**A**, **B**, **C** or **D**) which you think fits best according to the text.

Mark your answers **on the separate answer sheet**.

The Isle of Muck

Jim Richardson visits the Scottish island of Muck.

Lawrence MacEwen crouches down on his Scottish island, the Isle of Muck. And so do I. An Atlantic gale threatens to lift and blow us both out like October leaves, over the steep cliff at our feet and across the bay 120 m below, dropping us in the surrounding ocean. Then MacEwen's sheepdog, Tie, creeps up and his blond, bearded owner strokes him with gentle hands. The howling wind, rage as it might, can't make this man uncomfortable here, on his island, where he looks – and is – perfectly at home.

MacEwen is giving me a visual tour of his neighbourhood. Nodding to the north, he yells, 'That island is Eigg. The one to the west of it is the Isle of Rum. It gets twice as much rain as we do.' I watch heavy clouds dump rain on its huge mountains. 'Just beyond Rum is the island of Soay.' 'I have sheep to move,' MacEwen abruptly announces when rain drifts towards us. We start down the slopes. As we stride along, he brings me up to speed on island details: Volcanic Muck is 3 km long and half as wide; its geese eat vast amounts of grass; and the MacEwens have been living here for 3,000 years.

Herding the sheep interrupts the flow of information. Tie, the sheepdog, is circling a flock of sheep – and not doing it well. 'Away to me, Tie. *Away to me*,' meaning the dog should circle to the right. He doesn't; he goes straight up the middle of the flock, creating confusion. 'Tie.' MacEwen's voice drips disappointment. 'That will never do.' The dog looks ashamed.

The Isle of Muck is largely a MacEwen enterprise. Lawrence runs the farm with his wife, Jenny; son Colin, newly married, manages the island cottages; and daughter Mary runs the island hotel, Port Mor, with her husband, Toby. Mary and Toby love the fact that their two boys can wander the island on their own and sail dinghies on summer days. 'They go out of the door and come back only when they're hungry.' But island life has its compromises. For one, electricity is only available part of the time. My first evening, I wait anxiously for the lights to turn on. The next morning I find Mary setting out breakfast by torchlight. But I cope with it – along with no mobile phone service. 'There is mobile reception on the hill,' Mary tells me. 'Most visitors try for a couple of days, then just put the phone in the drawer.' So I do too.

Everything on Muck seems delightfully improbable. The boat today brings over the post – and three musicians, who hop off carrying instruments. Their concert in the island's tearoom proves a smash hit, with the islanders present tapping their boots in time to the music. That night, sitting by a glowing fire as it rains outside, Lawrence MacEwen tells me how he met his wife, Jenny. 'Her father saw a small farm on the isle of Soay advertised in the newspaper, and bought it without even looking at it. He'd never been to Scotland. Jenny was sent to manage it.' Did Jenny know anything about running a farm? 'She had good typing skills.'

I go to bed with rain and awake to more rain. But I eat well, virtually every bit of food coming from the tiny island. Mary sends me down to fisherman Sandy Mathers for fresh fish. I carry it back through the village and deliver it to Mary at the kitchen door. By 7 pm, our fish is on the table, delicious beyond reckoning. Also beyond reckoning: my ferry ride the following morning to my next island. Over the preceding two months, many of the scheduled ferries had been cancelled because of high seas. If my ferry didn't come, I'd be stuck on Muck for two more days. Which, now, phone or no phone, was *line 75* what I secretly longed for.

31 Why does the writer describe MacEwen stroking his dog?

    A to emphasise how bad MacEwen thought the weather was that day
    B to show the dog was as frightened by the storm as MacEwan was
    C to explain why MacEwen had risked going to the dangerous cliffs
    D to demonstrate how relaxed MacEwen was despite the bad weather

32 According to the writer, the sheepdog's behaviour suggests that

    A it never obeys MacEwen.
    B it is afraid of MacEwen.
    C it is aware it should have done better.
    D it usually responds to loud commands.

33 What is suggested about island life in the fourth paragraph?

    A People living there would like more visitors to help the economy.
    B People come to the island in search of employment.
    C People are too busy to do all the things they'd like to.
    D People don't mind putting up with some inconveniences.

34 What attitude is expressed by the writer in the fifth paragraph?

    A He is amused that people on the island share their feelings so openly.
    B He likes the way so many surprising things can happen on the island.
    C He approves of the way the islanders all socialise together.
    D He finds it strange that island farms are advertised in national newspapers.

35 What does 'Which' refer to in line 75?

    A the writer's ferry ride
    B the next island
    C having to stay on the island
    D a mobile phone

36 From the text as a whole, we find out the island of Muck

    A is a safe place for children to live.
    B has the highest level of rainfall in the area.
    C has an economy based solely on sheep.
    D is dependent on the outside world for its food.

Part 6

You are going to read a newspaper article about the Hollywood sign in the United States of America. Six sentences have been removed from the article. Choose from the sentences **A–H** the one which fits each gap (**37–42**). There is one extra sentence which you do not need to use.

Mark your answers **on the separate answer sheet**.

The sign on a hill

At the top of a hill called Mount Lee in Los Angeles on the west coast of the USA is a very famous sign, recognisable to people around the world. My job is to look after this sign. It says *Hollywood* and that's of course the place where films have been made for over a hundred years. The first film was made there in 1907 and by 1912, at least 15 independent studios could be found making films around town.

The film industry continued to grow and the name Hollywood, which by the 1920s represented not just a city but also an industry and a lifestyle, was made official when the 'Hollywoodland' sign was erected in 1923. It was only supposed to last about a year. **37** But it wasn't always. It started out as a massive billboard advertising an upscale suburban development called Hollywoodland.

In the 1940s, TV started to become popular and some Hollywood film studios closed, but then TV companies moved in and took them over. At this point, the city of Los Angeles decided to renovate the sign. The letters spelling 'land' were removed and the rest was repaired. Modern Hollywood was born. The letters in the sign weren't straight and still aren't. **38** They follow the shape of Mount Lee and this is part of their fame.

I am responsible for maintaining and protecting the sign. **39** When I first arrived in 1989, security was pretty low-tech – we put up a fence around the sign to stop trespassers messing with it. But people just jumped over the fence. The back of the sign was black with graffiti – there was barbed wire across it, but they still got through. So I decided to improve the effectiveness of the security.

Now we have motion-detectors and cameras. Everything goes via the internet to a dedicated surveillance team watching various structures around the city. **40** But they can get a closer look on one of my regular tours.

It's also important to protect the sign's image as it's used in loads of adverts and news pieces. There's a simple rule about how the sign can be used. **41** However, it mostly comes down to the look. To take a different example, if you used 'Hollywood' in the name of your company it would depend what the word looked like, whether it was just spelled out or whether the image of the sign itself was used.

People call up with the most ridiculous ideas. They want to light the sign, paint it pink, or cover it in something to promote their product. You'll get a really enthusiastic marketing executive call up, terribly excited because they think they're the first person to think of this or that idea. **42** That's because we don't like to change the image and we hope it will have the same significance for generations to come.

A Even so, people still try to climb over the barrier, mostly innocent tourists surprised that you can't walk right up to the sign.

B They mostly get turned down.

C If one of them ever fell down I would have to put it back up at exactly the same angle.

D We used to have real problems.

E Things have changed a lot since then.

F It's still there, of course, and is a symbol of the entertainment world.

G If the purpose is commercial – to promote something – payment has to be made.

Part 7

You are going to read an article in which four athletes talk about what they eat. For questions **43–52**, choose from the athletes (**A–D**). The athletes may be chosen more than once.

Mark your answers **on the separate answer sheet**.

Which athlete

enjoys cooking but finds the planning difficult?	43
has to carry food with him when training?	44
doesn't find it easy to eat before an event?	45
uses cooking as a way to relax?	46
sometimes allows himself certain food as a reward?	47
has seen a change in the diet of sports people?	48
once made the wrong decision about the food he ate?	49
says that people are unaware of what he actually eats?	50
says knowing what and when to eat is critical?	51
has had to change his diet with a change of sport?	52

Sports diets

Four athletes talk about what they eat.

A Mark

When I'm cycling on my own I stuff my pockets with bananas and protein bars. On the longest rides I'll eat something every half an hour. For heavier training it's physically impossible to get enough energy from food alone, so you do rely on energy drinks. One development in sports nutrition since I've been competing is the focus on the importance of protein. Cycling is much more weight-orientated than the swimming I used to do, which means I need to eat differently now. Protein feeds the muscles but keeps them as lean as possible. I've been an athlete for 20 years so healthy eating is normal for me, but that's not to say I don't get a tasty take-away meal from time to time. I've just learned to spot the meals that will provide what I need. It's simple things like steering clear of the creamy sauces and making sure I get lots of veg.

B Stefan

Everyone says: 'As a runner you must be on a really strict diet. Do you only eat salad? Are you allowed chocolate?' But that's really not the case. I've got salad and vegetables in my shopping trolley but there's always some chocolate in there, too. I do most of the cooking at home. On the morning of a competition, I get so nervous I feel really sick. I have to force myself to have something so I'll have enough energy to perform well. Sometimes I get those days where I don't want to be so disciplined. You think: 'I've trained really hard, I deserve to have a pizza.' It's OK to have a little relapse every now and then but I can't do it every day or I'd be rolling round the track!

C Guy

For a gymnast, a kilo can make all the difference. But if you don't eat enough you'll be a bit shaky and weak. It's all about eating the right amount, at the right time – two hours before you do anything. Breakfast is fruit and if I'm a bit peckish, wholewheat toast and butter! I get to training for 12 pm, then break after three hours for lunch – more fruit, a cheese and tomato sandwich. I'm back in the gym from 5 pm to 8 pm, then I go to my Mum's for steak and vegetables or chicken and salad. I don't tend to mix carbs with meat late at night. I'm not the best cook, but I think it's fun to do. I know how to make chicken from my mum's recipe, it just takes me a bit longer to get organised.

D Tomas

It's definitely possible to eat delicious food and be a professional swimmer. I've always loved food so I'm not going to be obsessive because you can get what you need and still enjoy every bite. I'm not really one for endless protein shakes and energy drinks. Before a training session I'd rather have a banana. That's not to say I'm perfect. At the world championships I got my feeding strategy wrong – and I paid for it. For my sport it's what you eat two days before the competition that makes the difference. You have to 'carb load' – eat piles of rice or pasta – and I didn't. I was leading for a long way but I ended up 11th. My biggest indulgence is pastry. And I love baking. I train for 33 hours a week so in my time off I need to rest, and spending time in the kitchen is perfect. Swimming is my biggest passion but baking comes a close second.

WRITING (1 hour 20 minutes)

Part 1

You **must** answer this question. Write your answer in **140–190** words in an appropriate style **on the separate answer sheet**.

---

1 In your English class you have been talking about relationships. Now, your English teacher has asked you to write an essay.

Write an essay using **all** the notes and give reasons for your point of view.

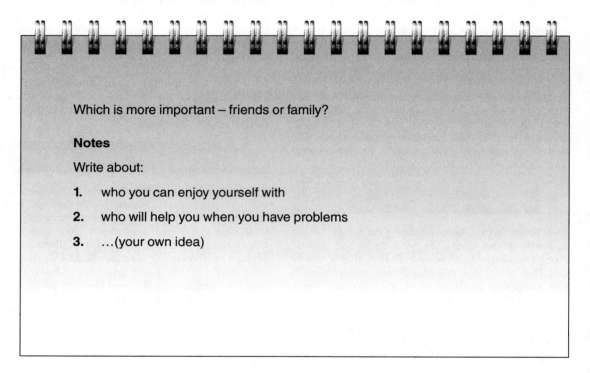

Which is more important – friends or family?

Notes

Write about:

1. who you can enjoy yourself with

2. who will help you when you have problems

3. …(your own idea)

Write your **essay**. You must use grammatically correct sentences with accurate spelling and punctuation in a style appropriate for the situation.

Part 2

Write an answer to **one** of the questions **2–4** in this part. Write your answer in **140–190** words in an appropriate style **on the separate answer sheet**. Put the question number in the box at the top of the answer sheet.

2   You recently saw this notice on an English-language website called Book World.

Reviews wanted!

The best thriller I have ever read!

Have you read a thriller recently that you think other readers would enjoy?
Write us a review of the book. You should include information on:

- what it's about
- why it's exciting
- who you would recommend it to.

The best reviews will be posted on the website next month.

Write your **review**.

3   You see this announcement on an English-language website.

Write your **article**.

ARTICLES WANTED

The most interesting weekend of my life

Write us an article about the most interesting weekend of your life. Explain what happened and where, and why it was so interesting.

The best articles will be posted on our website.

4   You have received this email from your English-speaking friend, Kim.

It's really kind of you to let me stay at your flat while you're on holiday. Please could you let me know how to get the keys? And could you also tell me anything else I need to know about the flat and whether there's anywhere near that I can buy food?

Thanks, Kim

Write your **email**.

LISTENING (approximately 40 minutes)

Part 1

You will hear people talking in eight different situations. For questions **1–8**, choose the best answer (**A**, **B** or **C**).

1   You hear a man talking about how his business became successful.
Where did his additional funding come from?

    A   the local bank

    B   a family friend

    C   his own savings

2   You hear a woman talking about a journey.
How did she travel?

    A   by boat

    B   by train

    C   by coach

3   You overhear a man talking to his wife on the phone.
What is he talking about?

    A   buying a car

    B   booking a holiday

    C   moving abroad

4   You hear two students talking about their course.
What does the woman think about the course?

    A   It is quite difficult.

    B   It is worth doing.

    C   It is becoming more interesting.

5 You hear a woman talking about roller derby, a hobby which involves speed racing on skates.
   What is she doing?

   A explaining what made her decide to take it up

   B appreciating her friends' attitude to the sport

   C describing how she feels when she's taking part

6 You hear part of a radio programme.
   What is the woman talking about?

   A a new shop

   B a new exhibition

   C a new leisure centre

7 You overhear two students discussing a reading project they did with young children.
   What do they agree about it?

   A The venue was perfect.

   B The material was well received.

   C The number of participants was surprising.

8 You hear an actor talking about the character she plays in a TV drama series.
   How does she feel about the character?

   A She is envious of her life-style.

   B She sympathises with her current problems.

   C She admires her intelligence.

Part 2

You will hear a woman called Gina Purvis, who is a pilot for a commercial airline, talking about her job. For questions **9–18**, complete the sentences with a word or short phrase.

_____

Sky high

Gina disliked her first job as a [9].

The airline that Gina works for insists on at least [10]

hours of flying experience from their captains.

Gina says that because her husband is a [11] he is

tolerant of her job.

The 'Notices to Pilots' provides information about any [12]

that are experiencing problems.

Gina says that if she has extra [13] she will need more fuel

for her flight.

Gina explains that many pilots she works with did a degree in

[14] at university.

Gina says that all the [15] must be within reach of the two

pilots in the cockpit.

The pilots look at a [16] to check if anyone is standing

at the cockpit entrance.

Gina gets information from a [17] about any small

problems on the plane.

Gina says what she really appreciates is a [18] flight.

Part 3

You will hear five short extracts in which students are talking about a trip they have taken. For questions **19–23**, choose from the list (**A–H**) what each student says about their trip. Use the letters only once. There are three extra letters which you do not need to use.

___

A   Someone I met while I was there is coming to visit me soon.

B   I plan to do things a little differently on my next visit.

Speaker 1		19

C   I learnt more about some friends while I was with them.

Speaker 2		20

D   I enjoyed myself thanks to one person's efforts.

Speaker 3		21

E   My experience was different when I returned to a place.

Speaker 4		22

F   Some people there offered to take me on a tour.

Speaker 5		23

G   I didn't take to the city at first.

H   I went back to a place I had never expected to see again.

Part 4

You will hear an interview with a musician called Jarrold Harding, who's talking about his career. For questions **24–30**, choose the best answer (**A**, **B** or **C**).

24 How did Jarrold's interest in music begin?

   A He went to one of his father's concerts.

   B He was given lessons by an orchestra violinist.

   C He watched musicians practising.

25 Jarrold played in his first concert

   A together with his mother.

   B when he was away on holiday with his parents.

   C to make his father happy.

26 What impressed Jarrold about his mother's musical ability?

   A She never made any mistakes.

   B She could memorise music very quickly.

   C She could adapt piano music for his violin.

27 What does Jarrold say about his interest in conducting?

   A It began at an early age.

   B It was encouraged by his father.

   C It increased when he heard famous musicians.

28 How did Jarrold feel when he was at college?

   A relieved to find he didn't have to work too hard

   B pleased at how well he played compared to everyone else

   C glad he could cope with things that some students struggled with

29 What did Jarrold do after leaving college?

    A He tried to devote all his time to conducting.

    B He was introduced to a good conducting teacher.

    C He had lessons with a famous conductor.

30 Jarrold thinks that being both a violinist and a conductor

    A has given him opportunities to develop as a musician.

    B has allowed him more freedom to play where he wants.

    C has earned him the respect of other professionals.

SPEAKING (14 minutes)

You take the Speaking test with another candidate (possibly two candidates), referred to here as your partner. There are two examiners. One will speak to you and your partner and the other will be listening. Both examiners will award marks.

Part 1 (2 minutes)

The examiner asks you and your partner questions about yourselves. You may be asked about things like 'your home town', 'your interests', 'your career plans', etc.

Part 2 (a one-minute 'long turn' for each candidate, plus a 30-second response from the second candidate)

The examiner gives you two photographs and asks you to talk about them for one minute. The examiner then asks your partner a question about your photographs and your partner responds briefly.

Then the examiner gives your partner two different photographs. Your partner talks about these photographs for one minute. This time the examiner asks you a question about your partner's photographs and you respond briefly.

Part 3 (4 minutes)

The examiner asks you and your partner to talk together. You may be asked to solve a problem or try to come to a decision about something. For example, you might be asked to decide the best way to use some rooms in a language school. The examiner gives you some text to help you but does not join in the conversation.

Part 4 (4 minutes)

The examiner asks some further questions, which leads to a more general discussion of what you have talked about in Part 3. You may comment on your partner's answers if you wish.

Test 3

READING AND USE OF ENGLISH (1 hour 15 minutes)

Part 1

For questions **1–8**, read the text below and decide which answer (**A**, **B**, **C** or **D**) best fits each gap. There is an example at the beginning (**0**).

Mark your answers **on the separate answer sheet**.

Example:

0　**A** inviting　　**B** attracting　　**C** involving　　**D** appealing

0	A	B	C	D
	▬	▭	▭	▭

New words for a dictionary

The editors of a new online dictionary are **(0)** ……… the public to submit words that they would like to see in the dictionary. People are already sending in words, some of which they have **(1)** ……… themselves – these will almost certainly not **(2)** ……… in the dictionary!

When a new word is submitted, editors check newspapers, radio, television and social networks to see how **(3)** ……… the word is used. They also **(4)** ……… whether the word is likely to remain in use for more than one or two years. The evidence they collect will help them decide whether or not to put it in the dictionary.

Editors will **(5)** ……… feedback on any words submitted by the public. Even words not accepted will **(6)** ……… to be monitored over the following year. Editors need to be **(7)** ……… of new words which emerge from areas such as popular culture and technology, so that their dictionary is a genuine **(8)** ……… of the current language.

1	**A** set out	**B** made up	**C** brought out	**D** come up
2	**A** include	**B** show	**C** consist	**D** appear
3	**A** totally	**B** widely	**C** fully	**D** vastly
4	**A** consider	**B** regard	**C** prove	**D** rate
5	**A** state	**B** tell	**C** provide	**D** inform
6	**A** keep	**B** rest	**C** last	**D** continue
7	**A** familiar	**B** aware	**C** alert	**D** experience
8	**A** mark	**B** copy	**C** reflection	**D** imitation

Part 2

For questions **9–16**, read the text below and think of the word which best fits each gap. Use only **one** word in each gap. There is an example at the beginning (**0**).

Write your answers **IN CAPITAL LETTERS on the separate answer sheet**.

Example: | **0** | | *I* | *S* | | | | | | | | | | | | | | | | | |

Animal communication

It **(0)** .... sometimes said that animals use language. Certainly some animal species have developed amazingly sophisticated ways of communicating with **(9)** .... another.

But there are huge differences between the ways animals communicate and the ways human beings do. When animals make a sound, such **(10)** .... a bark or a call, it is in reaction to **(11)** .... is happening around them. An alarm call means they are frightened. A hunger call means they want food. Animals, though, cannot make a call meaning 'I was scared yesterday' or 'I'll be hungry tomorrow'. Only human beings are capable **(12)** .... doing this.

Zoologists have had some success in teaching human language to animals. **(13)** .... some famous experiments, chimpanzees have **(14)** .... taught to use their hands to give information on a range of things. Some animals have even managed to put signs together in **(15)** .... to make simple sentences. However, getting them to do this takes a huge **(16)** .... of training.

Part 3

For questions **17–24**, read the text below. Use the word given in capitals at the end of some of the lines to form a word that fits in the gap **in the same line**. There is an example at the beginning **(0)**.

Write your answers **IN CAPITAL LETTERS on the separate answer sheet**.

Example: | 0 | C | Y | C | L | I | S | T | | | | | | | | | | |

Cycling

I have been a keen **(0)** .... for about nine years. When I began cycling,   **CYCLE**

I found the flat roads easy but the hills almost **(17)** .... Surprisingly,   **POSSIBLE**

now it's the opposite. A long flat ride can be both dull and **(18)** ....   **EXHAUST**

as you never experience that fantastic feeling of freedom when speeding

downhill. Years ago, going uphill left me **(19)** .... Now I have learned   **BREATH**

to take hills slowly and steadily.

When I set off, I'm full of energy and the first hundred metres are

(20) ...., the next couple of kilometres a bit tiring, but on the whole the   **MARVEL**

experience is very **(21)** ....   **ENJOY**

Cycling is **(22)** .... any other forms of exercise I have tried; it is never   **LIKE**

a chore but always a **(23)** .... The physical benefits are obvious but   **PLEASE**

the mental benefits are **(24)** .... important; when you are travelling   **EQUAL**

calmly at a sensible speed, you breathe fresh air, have time to think and

can relax.

Part 4

For questions **25–30**, complete the second sentence so that it has a similar meaning to the first sentence, using the word given. **Do not change the word given.** You must use between **two** and **five** words, including the word given. Here is an example (**0**).

Example:

0   A very friendly taxi driver drove us into town.

DRIVEN

We .... a very friendly taxi driver.

The gap can be filled by the words 'were driven into town by', so you write:

Example:	**0**	*WERE DRIVEN INTO TOWN BY*

Write **only** the missing words **IN CAPITAL LETTERS on the separate answer sheet**.

---

25   My brother doesn't play tennis now as well as he used to.

BETTER

My brother used to .... does now.

26   Clothing companies are selling an increasing number of goods on the internet.

BOUGHT

An increasing number of goods .... clothing companies on the internet.

27   'Well done for scoring twice, Mark,' said the coach.

PRAISED

Mark .... for scoring twice.

28 You are welcome to contact me if you need more information.

TOUCH

Please feel free .... me if you need more information.

29 Tickets for the concert cannot be bought before 12th May.

SALE

Tickets for the concert will not .... 12th May.

30 I didn't buy the camera because it was so expensive.

BEEN

I would have bought the camera .... so expensive.

Part 5

You are going to read part of an autobiography in which a gardener talks about his childhood and his love of plants and the countryside. For questions **31–36**, choose the answer (**A**, **B**, **C** or **D**) which you think fits best according to the text.

Mark your answers **on the separate answer sheet**.

Green fingers

It never occurred to me when I was little that gardens were anything less than glamorous places. Grandad's garden was on the bank of a river and sloped gently down towards the water. You couldn't reach the river but you could hear the sound of the water and the birds that sang in the trees above. I imagined that all gardens were like this – a place of escape, peace and solitude. Grandad's plot was nothing out of the ordinary when it came to features. He had nothing as grand as a greenhouse, unlike some of his neighbours. Not that they had proper 'bought' greenhouses. Theirs were made from old window frames. Patches of plastic would be tacked in place where a carelessly wielded spade had smashed a pane of glass.

At home, his son, my father, could be quiet and withdrawn. I wouldn't want to make him sound humourless. He wasn't. Silly things would amuse him. He had phrases that he liked to use, 'It's immaterial to me' being one of them. 'I don't mind' would have done just as well but he liked the word 'immaterial'. I realise that, deep down, he was probably disappointed that he hadn't made more of his life. He left school without qualifications and became apprenticed to a plumber. Plumbing was not something he was passionate about. It was just what he did. He was never particularly ambitious, though there was a moment when he and Mum
line 14 thought of emigrating to Canada, but it came to nothing. Where he came into his own was around the house. He had an 'eye for the job'. Be it bookshelves or a cupboard – what he could achieve was astonishing.

My parents moved house only once in their entire married life. But my mother made up for this lack of daring when it came to furniture. You would just get used to the shape of one chair when another appeared, but the most dramatic change of all was the arrival of a piano. I always wanted to like it but it did its best to intimidate me. The only thing I did like about it were the two brass candlesticks that jutted out from the front. 'They're too posh', my mother said and they disappeared one day while I was at school. There was never any mention of my being allowed to play it. Instead lessons were booked for my sister. When I asked my mother in later life why I wasn't given the opportunity, her reply was brief: 'You'd never have practised'.

Of the three options, moors, woods or river – the river was the one that usually got my vote. On a stretch of the river I was allowed to disappear with my imagination into another world. With a fishing net over my shoulder I could set off in sandals that were last year's model, with the fronts cut out to accommodate toes that were now right to the end. I'd walk along the river bank looking for a suitable spot where I could take off the painful sandals and leave them with my picnic while I ventured out, tentatively, peering through the water for any fish that I could scoop up with the net and take home. After the first disastrous attempts to keep them alive in the back yard, they were tipped back into the water.

I wanted to leave school as soon as possible but that seemed an unlikely prospect until one day my father announced, 'They've got a vacancy for an apprentice gardener in the Parks Department. I thought you might be interested.' In one brief moment Dad had gone against his better judgement. He might still have preferred it if I became a carpenter. But I like to feel that somewhere inside him was a feeling that things might just turn out for the best. If I stuck at it. Maybe I'm deceiving myself, but I prefer to believe that in his heart, although he hated gardening himself, he'd watched me doing it for long enough and noticed my unfailing passion for all things that grew and flowered and fruited.

31 When the writer describes his grandad's garden, he is

    A proud that his granddad was such a good gardener.
    B embarrassed that the garden was not as good as others nearby.
    C indignant that items in the garden were often damaged.
    D positive about the time he spent in the garden.

32 What is the writer's attitude to his father in the second paragraph?

    A regretful that his father had not achieved more
    B irritated that his father used words he didn't understand
    C sympathetic to the reasons why his father behaved as he did
    D grateful that his father had not taken the family to Canada

33 What does the writer mean by the phrase 'came into his own' in line 14?

    A was able to do something by himself
    B was able to show how talented he was
    C was able to continue his day job
    D was able to forget his failures

34 What was the writer's first reaction to the piano?

    A surprise when it suddenly appeared
    B pleasure at seeing it in the living room
    C anger that only his sister would have piano lessons
    D pride that his mother had listened to his advice

35 The writer's description of his fishing trips illustrate

    A how much free time he was given.
    B how beautiful the river was.
    C how good a fisherman he was.
    D how carefree his childhood was.

36 What is the main idea of the last paragraph?

    A His father did not want his son to be a gardener.
    B His father was tired of disagreeing with his son.
    C His father had been impressed by his son's love of gardening.
    D His father had been trying to find a job his son would enjoy.

Part 6

You are going to read an article about the experience of running while listening to music. Six sentences have been removed from the article. Choose from the sentences **A–G** the one which fits each gap (**37–42**). There is one extra sentence which you do not need to use.

Mark your answers **on the separate answer sheet**.

Does music make you run faster?

Runner Adharanand Finn took part in an unusual race in order to test the theory that music can make you run faster.

An expert on the effects of music on exercise, Dr Costas Karageorghis, claims that listening to music while running can boost performance by up to 15%. To put this theory to the test, I took part in a special Rock 'n' Roll half marathon, which had groups of musicians playing at various points along the route.

As I lined up at the start with almost 4,000 other runners, a singer sang an inspiring song for us. It may explain why I got off to a good start. I only came eighth in the end, though, even though I'd just spent six months training hard. **37** However, it turns out that all the training may have affected my response to the music; according to the research, the benefits of listening to music decrease with the level of intensity of the running.

'Elite athletes,' says Karageorghis, 'tend to focus inwardly when they are running.' According to him, most other runners look for stimulus and distraction from what is going on around them. 'Judging by your time,' he says, 'you are one of the former.' It is true. Apart from the song at the start, when I was standing still, I can barely remember the music played along the course. The first act I passed, a folk group, made me smile, and at one point I found myself running in time to the beat of some hard rock. **38** I can't say they helped my performance very much. But what did other runners make of the music?

Adam Bull usually runs marathons with no music and little crowd support. '**39** With the upbeat bands, you find yourself running to the beat, which helps. It also brings out people to cheer you on.' Rosie Bradford was also a convert. 'As we ran past one band and they started playing *These Boots Were Made for Walking*, everybody suddenly went faster.'

The only person I found who was less than happy with the music was Lois Lloyd. 'There wasn't enough of it, and I found it wasn't loud enough, so I ran with an MP3 player.' she said. '**40** ' Karageorghis is not surprised when I tell him. 'There are many advantages to using your own player, rather than relying on the music on the course,' he says. 'It gives you a constant stimulus, rather than just an occasional one, and you can tailor the playlist to your taste.'

One runner told me there was a direct correlation between the quality of the music on the course and how much it helped. But quality, of course, is subjective. I remember feeling annoyed as I ran past one band playing *Keep On Running*. **41**

Of course, the music was not only there to help runners break their personal bests (although sadly it was unable to help me beat mine), but to provide a sense of occasion, draw out the crowds and create a carnival atmosphere. **42** As I left, people were beginning to relax after the run, listening to an excellent rock band. It was a fitting way to end the day.

A I need my music all the time.

B I think they knew why I found the music here so distracting.

C I enjoyed that for a few moments, but both of them came and went in a flash.

D Along with some spring sunshine, it certainly achieved that.

E Someone else, though, may have found it uplifting.

F I was, in fact, taking my running pretty seriously at that time.

G The music here has been great for my performance.

Part 7

You are going to read four reviews of a science documentary series on TV. For questions **43–52**, choose from the reviews (**A–D**). The reviews may be chosen more than once.

Mark your answers **on the separate answer sheet**.

___

In which review does it say that

an effort was made to connect a number of unrelated issues?	**43**
the topics covered are well chosen?	**44**
viewers are shown how science can occasionally do better than nature?	**45**
the series deals with something people have hoped to achieve for a while?	**46**
the series unfortunately didn't spend a lot of time explaining the topics covered?	**47**
viewers are clearly informed?	**48**
it's good that viewers are not required to consider all aspects of the subject carefully?	**49**
the series was worth making despite the topic not appearing very interesting at first?	**50**
viewers may not always find the series comfortable to watch?	**51**
the series achieves its aims by astonishing its viewers?	**52**

Reviews of TV science documentary series

Paul Hansen looks at the latest science programmes.

A Science for All

Fortunately for me and non-scientists everywhere, the makers of *Science for All* are there to plug the gaps in our knowledge. The series is rather like a knowledgeable parent who doesn't mind being pestered by wide-eyed and curious children: it takes the time to explain all those fascinating mysteries of nature in an entertaining and understandable way. The last series opened my eyes to all manner of interesting facts and demystified some of the problems faced by modern physics. And the new series shows no lack of inspiration for subjects to tackle: everything from the existence of life on other planets to the odd properties of human memory are rightly considered suitable subjects. So, while it's a shame that factual programmes are getting increasingly scarce these days, it's a comfort that *Science for All* shows no signs of dipping in quality or disappearing from public view.

B Out in Space

Although I wasn't expecting much from this series, I'm pleased that the producers of *Out in Space* persisted with their unpromising subject. In the course of the first programme we learn about hurricanes, deserts, and even how the Moon was made; a bewildering mix of phenomena that, we were assured, were all caused by events beyond our planet's atmosphere. That's not to say the programme explored them in any great detail, preferring to skip breathlessly from one to the next. The essential logic of the series seemed to be that if you take any natural phenomenon and ask 'why?' enough times, the answers will eventually be that it's something to do with space. The two presenters attempted to get it all to fit together, by taking part in exciting activities. Sadly these only occasionally succeeded.

C Stars and Planets

The second series of *Stars and Planets* is an attempt to take advantage of the success of the first, which unexpectedly gained a substantial general audience. Like its predecessor, this is big on amazing photography and fabulous graphics, most of which are much less successful at communicating the immensity of the ideas involved than one human being talking to you directly. This time the scope is even wider, astronomically speaking. What we are being introduced to here are ambitious ideas about time and space, and the presenter succeeds rather better than you might expect. It helps that he doesn't go too deep, as once you start thinking about it this is tricky stuff to get your head around. The point of such programmes is less to explain every detail than to arouse a generalised sense of amazement that might lead to further thinking, and *Stars and Planets* is certainly good at that.

D Robot Technology

This ground-breaking science documentary series follows a group of experts as they attempt to build a complete artificial human from robotic body parts. The project sees scientists use the latest technology from the world's most renowned research centres and manufacturers. It is the realisation of a long-held dream to create a human from manufactured parts, using everything from bionic arms and mechanical hearts, eye implants and microchip brains. The series explores to what extent modern technology is capable of replacing body parts – or even improving their abilities. The presenter, very appropriately, has an artificial hand himself. This ambitious series gives us a guided tour of the wonders of modern technology. Though it can be a slightly upsetting journey at times, it engages the audience in a revolution that is changing the face of medicine.

WRITING (1 hour 20 minutes)

Part 1

You **must** answer this question. Write your answer in **140–190** words in an appropriate style **on the separate answer sheet**.

---

1   In your English class you have been talking about work. Now, your English teacher has asked you to write an essay.

Write an essay using **all** the notes and give reasons for your point of view.

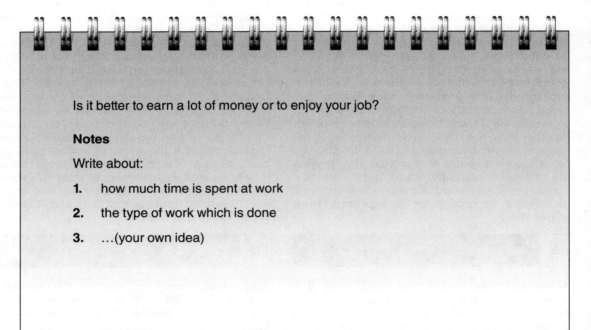

Is it better to earn a lot of money or to enjoy your job?

Notes

Write about:

1.   how much time is spent at work

2.   the type of work which is done

3.   …(your own idea)

Write your **essay**. You must use grammatically correct sentences with accurate spelling and punctuation in a style appropriate for the situation.

Part 2

Write an answer to **one** of the questions **2–4** in this part. Write your answer in **140–190** words in an appropriate style **on the separate answer sheet**. Put the question number in the box at the top of the answer sheet.

---

2   Your college would like to start an English-language film club where people can go to watch films in English and discuss them. Your English teacher has asked you to write a report giving your suggestions about:

- what type of films should be shown
- how often the film club should meet
- how the film club should be advertised.

Write your **report**.

3   You see this announcement on an English-language website.

ARTICLES WANTED

What does happiness mean to you?

Tell us about the kinds of things that make you feel happy, and why?

Write us an article answering these questions.

The best articles will be posted on our website.

Write your **article**.

4   You have seen this advertisement in your local English language newspaper.

Round the world trip – Travel Competition

Do you like adventure? Would you like a chance to travel?

We need one more person to join a small group on a trip around the world.

Write to Mrs Hopkins, the organizer of the trip, telling her:

- why you would like to go on the trip
- what skills you have which would be useful on the trip
- what previous experience you have of travelling (if any).

Write your **letter of application**.

LISTENING (approximately 40 minutes)

Part 1

You will hear people talking in eight different situations. For questions **1–8**, choose the best answer (**A**, **B** or **C**).

---

1 You hear a young actor talking about a colleague.
What does he say about her?

   A She makes acting seem easy.

   B She speaks very slowly.

   C She gives him good advice.

2 You hear two friends talking about a colleague.
What do they agree about?

   A how ambitious he is

   B how well-paid he is

   C how stressed he is

3 You hear an author talking about his new book.
What point is he making about it?

   A It will be widely read.

   B It took a long time to write.

   C It is better than his first book.

4 You hear two friends talking about something they saw on TV.
What did they see?

   A an advertisement

   B a comedy series

   C a documentary

5 You hear an office manager talking about her work.
How does she feel about it?

  A confident that she can do it well

  B interested in her new project

  C satisfied with her staff

6 You overhear two friends talking in a restaurant.
What do they agree about?

  A how reasonable the price is

  B how spicy the food is

  C how varied the menu is

7 You hear a woman talking about her neighbours' holiday photographs.
What is she doing?

  A complaining about having to look at them

  B admiring her neighbours' photography skills

  C suggesting how they could be improved

8 You hear two friends talking about a concert they've just been to.
What did they find disappointing about it?

  A the poor sound quality

  B the seats they had booked

  C the lack of air conditioning

Part 2

You will hear a man called Henry Lee giving a talk about the first time he went skydiving. For questions **9–18**, complete the sentences with a word or short phrase.

My first jump

Henry had his first skydiving lesson in the month of [_____ **9**] .

Henry had to attend a talk about [_____ **10**] before his jump.

Henry says that a [_____ **11**] was the most important piece of equipment he was given.

Henry was surprised that the plane the club used didn't have any

[_____ **12**] in it.

Henry's instructor had jumped a total of [_____ **13**] times in the past.

Henry had brought some [_____ **14**] with him to wear during the jump.

Henry said he felt totally [_____ **15**] when the plane door was opened.

Henry uses the word [_____ **16**] to describe the winding river he could see below him.

Henry compares his landing to that of a [_____ **17**] landing on the ground.

Henry was pleased to be given a [_____ **18**] after his jump.

Part 3

You will hear five short extracts in which students are talking about the experience of living and studying away from home. For questions **19–23**, choose from the list (**A–H**) what each student says. Use the letters only once. There are three extra letters which you do not need to use.

A   I was much younger than the other people I lived with.

B   I'm still closest to the people I grew up with.

Speaker 1   [ ] **19**

C   I found that joining a sports club helped me make friends.

Speaker 2   [ ] **20**

D   I didn't share many interests with my classmates.

Speaker 3   [ ] **21**

E   It was easier making friends at a small college.

Speaker 4   [ ] **22**

F   It was hard getting out to make friends at first.

Speaker 5   [ ] **23**

G   I'm still in touch with the people I lived with at first.

H   It was good living with people who had similar interests.

Part 4

You will hear an interview with a student athlete called Chelsea Matthews, who plays soccer for her college. For questions **24–30**, choose the best answer (**A**, **B** or **C**).

---

24 What impact does playing soccer have on Chelsea's life?

    A She needs private tuition from her teachers.

    B She doesn't take part in some other student activities.

    C She never gets to travel to other countries.

25 Chelsea had to start planning to be a student athlete at 16 because

    A there were many requirements that had to be met.

    B there were few colleges that offered the course she wanted.

    C there was a lot of competition for places in good colleges.

26 Chelsea is happy to return to college a month early because

    A she is pleased at the prospect of starting competitions.

    B she feels relieved to get back into a routine.

    C she realises that training is necessary.

27 When Chelsea and her team-mates finish training, they

    A can take a break by going to the movies.

    B are too tired to do very much except sleep.

    C relax with other sports teams.

28 Chelsea says if she and her team-mates miss too many classes

    A they may get poor grades and have to leave the team.

    B their professors will complain to the head of faculty.

    C the other students are understanding about the reason for their absence.

29 What problem did Chelsea herself have in keeping up with her studies?

    A She was away sick for some of her classes.

    B She had to study one subject under difficult conditions.

    C She was expected to commit herself to extra training for away games.

30 In conclusion, what does Chelsea say about being a student athlete?

    A It has taught her the importance of aiming high.

    B It has helped her decide what her future career should be.

    C It has changed her perception of the value of friendship.

SPEAKING (14 minutes)

You take the Speaking test with another candidate (possibly two candidates), referred to here as your partner. There are two examiners. One will speak to you and your partner and the other will be listening. Both examiners will award marks.

Part 1 (2 minutes)

The examiner asks you and your partner questions about yourselves. You may be asked about things like 'your home town', 'your interests', 'your career plans', etc.

Part 2 (a one-minute 'long turn' for each candidate, plus a 30-second response from the second candidate)

The examiner gives you two photographs and asks you to talk about them for one minute. The examiner then asks your partner a question about your photographs and your partner responds briefly.

Then the examiner gives your partner two different photographs. Your partner talks about these photographs for one minute. This time the examiner asks you a question about your partner's photographs and you respond briefly.

Part 3 (4 minutes)

The examiner asks you and your partner to talk together. You may be asked to solve a problem or try to come to a decision about something. For example, you might be asked to decide the best way to use some rooms in a language school. The examiner gives you some text to help you but does not join in the conversation.

Part 4 (4 minutes)

The examiner asks some further questions, which leads to a more general discussion of what you have talked about in Part 3. You may comment on your partner's answers if you wish.

Test 4

READING AND USE OF ENGLISH (1 hour 15 minutes)

Part 1

For questions **1–8**, read the text below and decide which answer (**A**, **B**, **C** or **D**) best fits each gap. There is an example at the beginning (**0**).

Mark your answers **on the separate answer sheet**.

Example:

0 **A** heart **B** key **C** bottom **D** focus

0	A	B	C	D
	▃	▁	▁	▁

Memory

Memory is at the **(0)** ……….. of our sense of personal identity. If we did not have memory, we would not be **(1)** ……….. of our relationships with other people and would have no **(2)** ……….. that we had had any past at all. And without memory we would have no knowledge on which to **(3)** ……….. our present and future.

Memory **(4)** ……….. of three processes: registration, retention and recall. Registration happens when we consciously notice something. Retention is the next **(5)** ……….. , when we keep something we have noticed in our minds for a certain period of time. Finally, recall occurs when we actively think about some of these things that are **(6)** ……….. in our minds.

Every day we are subjected to a vast **(7)** ……….. of information. If we remembered every **(8)** ……….. thing we had ever seen or heard, life would be impossible. Consequently, our brains have learnt to register only what is of importance.

1	**A** familiar	**B** aware	**C** informed	**D** acquainted
2	**A** view	**B** suggestion	**C** belief	**D** idea
3	**A** base	**B** depend	**C** do	**D** make
4	**A** contains	**B** involves	**C** includes	**D** consists
5	**A** action	**B** division	**C** set	**D** stage
6	**A** seated	**B** stocked	**C** stored	**D** sited
7	**A** level	**B** amount	**C** extent	**D** number
8	**A** exact	**B** single	**C** one	**D** isolated

Part 2

For questions **9–16**, read the text below and think of the word which best fits each gap. Use only **one** word in each gap. There is an example at the beginning (**0**).

Write your answers **IN CAPITAL LETTERS on the separate answer sheet.**

Example: | 0 | B | E | T | W | E | E | N | | | | | | | | | | |

Visit to a sweets factory

Today I am visiting a sweets factory, a building squeezed **(0)** ……... a railway line and a canal. **(9)** ……... I watch, trucks filled with sugar arrive at the factory where this family-owned company has been making sweets for some 80 years.

Being in a factory **(10)** ……... this one is exactly **(11)** ……... children dream of. I am staring at huge vats of sticky liquid **(12)** ……... eventually ends up as mouth-watering sweets. Every now **(13)** ……... then I see a factory worker in a white coat put a sweet into her mouth.

Ailsa Kelly, granddaughter of the company owner, remembers visiting the factory as **(14)** ……... child with her grandfather. 'He would take me onto the factory floor and introduce me,' she says. 'He told me, "You may work here some day." And indeed, she has, continuously, **(15)** ……... 1999. The sense of family is **(16)** ……... of the reasons employees are remarkably loyal to the company.

Part 3

For questions **17–24**, read the text below. Use the word given in capitals at the end of some of the lines to form a word that fits in the gap **in the same line**. There is an example at the beginning (**0**).

Write your answers **IN CAPITAL LETTERS on the separate answer sheet**.

Example: | 0 | N | E | R | V | O | U | S | | | | | | | | | |

Job interviews

Most people feel rather **(0)** .... when they go for an interview for a new   **NERVE**

job. This is not surprising as getting a job one wants is important. People

being interviewed expect the interviewers to be **(17)** .... , matching   **OBJECT**

an applicant against a job **(18)** .... However, what often happens in   **DESCRIBE**

reality is that the interviewers make **(19)** .... that are little more than   **DECIDE**

reactions to the **(20)** .... of the applicant.   **PERSON**

Even skilled interviewers may, without realising it, **(21)** .... favour   **CONSCIOUS**

people who make them feel at **(22)** .... With this in mind, if you go   **EASY**

for an interview you should try to make a good impression from the start

by presenting the interviewers with the very best version of yourself,

emphasising the **(23)** .... of skills you have. You must appear very   **VARY**

positive and as **(24)** .... as possible. It is for you to convince the   **ENTHUSIASM**

interviewers that you are definitely the most suitable person for the job.

Part 4

For questions **25–30**, complete the second sentence so that it has a similar meaning to the first sentence, using the word given. **Do not change the word given.** You must use between **two** and **five** words, including the word given. Here is an example (**0**).

Example:

0   A very friendly taxi driver drove us into town.

   DRIVEN

   We .... a very friendly taxi driver.

The gap can be filled by the words 'were driven into town by', so you write:

Example:	**0**	*WERE DRIVEN INTO TOWN BY*

Write **only** the missing words **IN CAPITAL LETTERS on the separate answer sheet**.

---

25   'Do you know the cost of the trips?' asked Pamela.

   MUCH

   Pamela asked if I knew .... were.

26   During the quiz, I could not think of the correct answer to the winning question.

   COME

   During the quiz, I was not .... the correct answer to the winning question.

27   I promised that I would think carefully about the job offer.

   GIVE

   I promised .... the job offer.

28 The group continued to walk despite rain starting to fall.

EVEN

The group carried .... started to rain.

29 Almost all the tickets for next Saturday's concert have been sold.

HARDLY

There are .... for next Saturday's concert.

30 Do you think it is likely that Peter will get the job he has applied for?

CHANCE

Do you think that Peter has .... the job he has applied for?

Part 5

You are going to read an article about the video games industry. For questions **31–36**, choose the answer (**A**, **B**, **C** or **D**) which you think fits best according to the text.

Mark your answers **on the separate answer sheet**.

A career in the video games industry?

Reporter Lauren Cope finds out about working in the video games industry.

Initially populated by computer scientists and the self-taught, the video game design industry used not to offer many routes into its midst. Often, perhaps unfairly, viewed as just a hobby for young enthusiasts, the video games industry is now being taken seriously. Surprised? Industry experts aren't.

It's not easy though. Video game spin-offs that rapidly follow any new movie require dozens of team members and months of incredible skill, perseverance and intricacies. As with almost every industry, it's tricky to get into – but it is expanding. Jim Donelly, a spokesman for an online games magazine says: 'It's certainly very difficult to make much headway within big companies, or to influence any of the really big mainstream games. But the truth is, the industry needs game designers more than ever. Not just director-level people who orchestrate an entire game, but the lower-level people who design systems and individual set pieces.'

So, how can you get into such a competitive industry? Although many companies prefer people to have a degree in computer science, Jim disagrees. 'There is only one route: make games. The tools are there. You won't get a job if you haven't made something, and you won't get anywhere independently if you are not making stuff. Game design is less a job than it is a way of life. Like any creative endeavour it must be done to be real.' Another industry expert, John Field, sees other options. 'There's a lot to be said for "just *line 32* doing it", but it's really more complicated than that. There are lots of people who want to work in games, but few who measure up to the requirements of the industry these days; even fewer who have the creative talent, technical know-how, vision and entrepreneurial ability to really contribute to the ever-changing face of an evolving medium.'

Can you do it on your own? 'Perhaps, but it's pretty tricky,' says John. 'However, a good postgraduate course in games can help, plus provide a year or two of top-level support and guidance. Most games designers start their careers as programmers, or artists, progressing their way up the ladder. They are interested in all forms of entertainment media, plus have a healthy appetite for all areas of the arts and contemporary culture. They may or may not have spent a few years in the working world post-graduation, but have realised that games is going to be their "thing". They are not merely fans, but are fascinated by the future possibilities of games, and are aware of the increasing breadth and diversity of the form. And finally connections can help. This is often overlooked, but in order to get *line 5* ahead in games – as in many other areas – you need to network.'

The childish stereotype of the adolescent boy glued to his games console has long been replaced by the more accurate perception of a grown-up medium, grabbing our attention. Families frequently get involved on interactive consoles. Smart phones introduce a wealth of new games through apps, as well as social media. John believes there is plenty of room for expansion. 'Games have become pervasive play-things for increasingly large audiences. They are also a great way to learn things and I see this already big area as an expanding array of possibilities and opportunities.'

31 What is the writer's main point about the video games industry in the first paragraph?

    A It is reasonable to consider making a living in this field.

    B Young people's contributions to it should be appreciated.

    C It offers a relatively limited number of career options.

    D Specialists in this area have failed to value its potential.

32 What does Jim tell us about the video games industry?

    A It can be hard to decide which idea will prove successful.

    B Many designers are required to take charge of each large project.

    C It is worth recognising the value of having a long-term strategy.

    D There is room for people with different degrees of responsibility.

33 What does 'that' refer to in line 32?

    A getting a degree in computer science

    B making games

    C being independent

    D seeing other options

34 What opinion does John express in the third paragraph?

    A It is a mistake to believe that the jobs people do in the industry are easy.

    B Many people lack the qualities needed to do effective work in the industry.

    C The industry could benefit from people who have a strong desire to work in it.

    D The industry is changing too rapidly for people to keep up with it.

35 What does 'overlooked' mean in line 54?

    A not considered

    B understood

    C not used

    D required

36 In the final paragraph, we are told that

    A video games have not been effectively exploited as learning tools.

    B young people are being offered more demanding games to play.

    C people used to misunderstand the true nature of video games.

    D other technologies have forced the games industry to compete.

Part 6

You are going to read part of the autobiography of David Coulthard, who is a retired Formula One racing driver. Six sentences have been removed from the autobiography. Choose from the sentences **A–G** the one which fits each gap (**37–42**). There is one extra sentence which you do not need to use.

Mark your answers **on the separate answer sheet**.

Grand Prix driver

I'm a great believer in success, in achieving whatever goal you set on a particular day, so whether I was practising on the track or working out in the gym, I always put my heart and soul into it.

When I was learning my trade, racing on karts as a teenager, I would look after my helmet and race suit carefully. Everything had to be perfect; it was all about preparation. At 18, I progressed to Formula Ford racing, a stage before Formula One, and I'd even get the car up in the garage and polish the underside until it was gleaming. **37** But I made the point, jokingly, that if I ever rolled over in a race, my car would have the shiniest underside in history.

It may be that the environment of Formula One fuelled this obsession with neatness and cleanliness. It's a profession based on precision and exactness. If you walk around a team factory it looks like a science laboratory. **38** A Formula One factory couldn't be further from that; it's like something from another planet.

Everything is aircraft standard and quality. And so it should be. If some mega-rich potential sponsor walks into a dirty factory to find people lounging around, that doesn't make a great impression. If they walk in and everyone's working hard and there's not a speck of dust anywhere, that's another matter. **39**

Polishing my helmet was a specific ritual I had. The race helmet is an important and prized possession. When you're starting out, you only have one helmet for several years and it can be a pricey piece of kit. **40** By the time you get to Formula One, you're getting through probably a dozen or more expensive ones a year. Normally I'd never have dreamed of wearing someone else's, but I did have a problem with the front of my helmet some years ago at the Monaco Grand Prix, and just couldn't see properly. In the end I used one belonging to Nelson Piquet.

He very kindly let me keep the helmet after the race. He'd finished second in the Brazilian Grand Prix with that helmet, so it's a unique piece of history – two drivers wearing the same helmet and finishing second in different races. Four years later, Nelson said he wanted to swap another helmet with me. This was before he'd announced he was retiring, so my immediate thought was, what's with this helmet collection thing? **41** There must be something in it. So I gave him a helmet and he gave me a signed one of his.

Helmets are treasured and it's quite rare for me to give race ones to anyone. I only gave my friend Richard one recently, although we've known each other since we were five. Sometimes it's easy to forget obvious things. **42** It should be the other way round.

A I certainly took good care of mine as a result.

B You take for granted those you're closest to and you make an effort with people you hardly know.

C But it was only natural for me to be so particular about cleanliness before racing.

D Think of a motor mechanic, and you think of oil and dirt, filthy overalls, grubby fingers.

E Some people said this was ridiculous because it wasn't as if anyone was ever going to see it.

F Perhaps I should be doing it as well.

G That's why all the teams try and compete hard with each other on presentation.

Part 7

You are going to read an article about four women who have recently worked as volunteers. For questions **43–52**, choose from the women (**A–D**). The women may be chosen more than once.

Mark your answers **on the separate answer sheet**.

Which volunteer

found that there was a wide choice of opportunities?	**43**
was very aware of all aspects of natural life around her?	**44**
was warned of a possible danger?	**45**
did not achieve her ambition quite as she had expected?	**46**
thought that she had gained as much as she had given?	**47**
was shown sympathy by someone on her project?	**48**
says her family had influenced her choice of work?	**49**
says she amazed herself by what she achieved?	**50**
appreciated the flexibility of her boss?	**51**
describes the difficulties posed by the environment she was in?	**52**

Volunteers

A — Teresa

For many years I had fantasised about spending December on a white, tropical beach on a remote island. I finally found my slice of paradise in the Seychelles when my dream came true last year, though not exactly in the way I had envisaged. I had been feeling burnt out from work and wanted to escape winter and learn new skills. Volunteer projects seemed a good option. Narrowing my search criteria to marine research helped cut down the thousands of options out there and I eventually joined a coral protection project to help determine the long-term impact of rising sea temperatures on the ecosystem. Within 24 hours of our group's arrival, we lived and breathed coral, not just under water but also in the camp – with 52 coral types to master and up to three research dives a day. If there was a downside, it was the seemingly endless chores in the camp, but I didn't mind. But the experience was, overall, incredible. I stretched myself beyond my wildest imagination.

B — Patricia

Imagine spending the summer as I did, working on the edge of an active volcano in Hawaii. I had once been on a ranger-guided walk there with my family. I had been terrified. However, as I relaxed I slowly realised that the ranger's job was something I'd like to do too. So a few years later I applied and got a volunteer ranger job. I found living there surprisingly laid back, as well as exciting. After a crash course in geology, I was given the volunteer ranger uniform and began the job. On the first morning I found myself in front of a group of visitors. Suddenly, I was the 'authority', delivering a talk on the volcanic past and present of the islands. As a volunteer I was making the park come alive for the visitors, and they in turn made Hawaii come alive for me.

C — Helen

After months of study, I wanted to get away for a bit. My dad is an artist and often does paintings of tropical birds. I'd always wanted to find out more about them. From the internet I found that a farm which breeds parrots was looking for volunteers. I arrived in the middle of a panic situation – a storm had knocked the electricity out, and the generator, needed for keeping the eggs warm, was nearly out of petrol. After visiting several garages we found some and dashed back just in time. I really enjoyed my stay. Some hosts lay down strict rules on the amount of work expected but luckily mine, Darryl, preferred to set out projects which he wanted my help with. Most of the time I did basic maintenance jobs and fed the birds. 'They can break coconuts with their beaks and they'll take your finger off so be careful,' Darryl advised. So, I chopped bananas and then used a long fork to pass the fruit in to the birds without risking my fingers.

D — Kate

During my stay in Guatemala, I volunteered to work on a plantation. One day, my supervisor, René inspected my scratched hands and asked gently if I needed gloves. I gathered my strength and told him that gloves might indeed help. Then I grasped my knife and resumed my attack on the invading roots that were constantly threatening to drag the fragile new cacao plantation back into the rainforest. In the sticky red earth, everything grows – the trouble is that it is rarely what you planted. Walking through the plantation, René had to point out to me the treasured cash crops of coffee, cacao and macadamias. To my eye, they were indistinguishable from the surrounding jungle. Every day I caught glimpses of little waterfalls and vividly coloured butterflies between towering bamboo. The air was always heavy with the sound of insects. It was a great experience.

WRITING (1 hour 20 minutes)

Part 1

You **must** answer this question. Write your answer in **140–190** words in an appropriate style **on the separate answer sheet**.

---

1   In your English class you have been talking about animals and the environment. Now, your English teacher has asked you to write an essay.

Write an essay using **all** the notes and give reasons for your point of view.

'We should do everything we can to save animals which are in danger of disappearing from our planet.' Do you agree?

Notes

Write about:

1.   the kind of animals which are in danger

2.   the reasons for protecting these animals

3.   … (your own idea)

Write your **essay**. You must use grammatically correct sentences with accurate spelling and punctuation in a style appropriate for the situation.

Part 2

Write an answer to **one** of the questions **2–4** in this part. Write your answer in **140–190** words in an appropriate style **on the separate answer sheet**. Put the question number in the box at the top of the answer sheet.

---

2   You see this announcement on an English-language website.

> **ARTICLES WANTED**
>
> ## What are the most important things for young children to learn?
>
> How to make friends? Telling the truth? Or something else? Write us an article saying what things you think are important for young children to learn, and why?
>
> The best articles will be posted on our website.

Write your **article**.

3   You recently saw this notice on an English-language website called Music Live.

> **Reviews Wanted!**
>
> ## A concert I've been to
>
> Write us a review of a concert you've been to. It could be a pop, rock or classical concert, or one with a different type of music. Include information on the music, the place and the atmosphere.
>
> The best reviews will be posted on the website next month.

Write your **review**.

4   A group of English students is coming to your college. Your English teacher has asked you to write a report on **one** local tourist attraction. In your report you should:

- describe the attraction
- say what you can do there
- explain why you think students would enjoy visiting it.

Write your **report**.

LISTENING (approximately 40 minutes)

Part 1

You will hear people talking in eight different situations. For questions **1–8**, choose the best answer (**A**, **B** or **C**).

---

1   You hear a sportsperson talking about her sporting career.
    What is she going to do in the future?

   A   change her career

   B   become a sports writer

   C   train for the next event

2   You hear two friends talking about a laboratory experiment.
    How do they both feel now?

   A   anxious about the procedures they used

   B   annoyed about having to repeat it

   C   disappointed with the results

3   You overhear a student calling his university department.
    Why is he phoning?

   A   to make a complaint

   B   to find out about a course

   C   to book an appointment

4   You hear two friends talking about a website.
    The man thinks that the website is

   A   helpful.

   B   interesting.

   C   easy to use.

5   You hear a man talking about his decision to become a singer.
His mother was unhappy about it because she didn't

   A   like his kind of music.

   B   want him to leave education.

   C   think it would suit him.

6   You overhear a man calling a TV shop.
Why is he calling?

   A   to cancel an order

   B   to arrange a delivery

   C   to make a purchase

7   You hear two friends talking about a meal.
What do they agree about it?

   A   It was expensive for the amount of food they got.

   B   Some of the foods they were served didn't go well together.

   C   The dishes they were given weren't cooked properly.

8   You hear a college lecturer talking to a student.
What is he doing?

   A   giving encouragement

   B   offering to help

   C   suggesting improvements

Part 2

You will hear a girl called Kyra talking about the badminton club she belongs to. For questions **9–18**, complete the sentences with a word or short phrase.

Badminton club

Before she took up badminton, | **9** | had been Kyra's

favourite sport.

People interested in joining the club are invited to what's called a

' | **10** | session.

Club committee members can be identified by the colour of their

| **11** | at sessions.

Members of the badminton club pay a membership fee of

£ | **12** | each year.

New badminton club members can use the | **13** |

at Sportsworld without paying.

When new members join the club, a | **14** | is given to them

as a free gift.

There is coaching for the club's | **15** | on a Monday evening.

Members can look at the club's | **16** | to see which

courts are free at Sportsworld.

The club's annual | **17** | is its most popular social event.

New badminton club members will be offered a | **18** |

at the Sportsworld café.

Part 3

You will hear five short extracts in which people are talking about why their businesses became successful. For questions **19–23**, choose from the list (**A–H**) what each speaker says. Use the letters only once. There are three extra letters which you do not need to use.

A   I don't need to employ anyone.

B   I decided to change the way I promoted the business.

Speaker 1	19

C   I took a business course.

Speaker 2	20

D   I was able to get financial backing.

Speaker 3	21

E   I believe in looking after my employees.

Speaker 4	22

F   I believe my business offers a unique service to customers.

Speaker 5	23

G   I learnt a lot from other business people.

H   I made changes because of customer feedback.

Part 4

You will hear a radio interview with a man called Tony Little, who makes wildlife films and works for a wildlife conservation organisation called The Nature Trust. For questions **24–30**, choose the best answer (**A**, **B** or **C**).

24 Tony thinks that the hardest challenge he faces is

    A to publicise what The Nature Trust does.

    B to expand the range of people volunteering.

    C to interest local groups in a variety of activities.

25 What does Tony think about the use of plastic?

    A He knows it will be difficult to change people's attitudes to it.

    B He worries that there is no way of preventing plastic waste.

    C He believes it causes the biggest problem to wildlife.

26 Tony hopes that his new website Nature Talk will help people learn

    A about different animal habitats.

    B how to watch animals in the wild.

    C which animals are endangered.

27 Tony says the achievement that he is most proud of is

    A helping to make a popular film.

    B doing a scientific study.

    C working on an award-winning project.

28 What disadvantage does Tony mention about having a career as a cameraman?

    A It is often badly paid.

    B It can be hard to find enough work.

    C It usually involves long hours.

29 Tony advises young naturalists that it is essential to have

    A suitable walking boots.

    B the latest photography equipment.

    C good binoculars.

30 What would Tony like to do in the future?

    A to help save the tiger and polar bear

    B to publicise the dangers facing a variety of species

    C to produce more films for TV about animals

SPEAKING (14 minutes)

You take the Speaking test with another candidate (possibly two candidates), referred to here as your partner. There are two examiners. One will speak to you and your partner and the other will be listening. Both examiners will award marks.

Part 1 (2 minutes)

The examiner asks you and your partner questions about yourselves. You may be asked about things like 'your home town', 'your interests', 'your career plans', etc.

Part 2 (a one-minute 'long turn' for each candidate, plus a 30-second response from the second candidate)

The examiner gives you two photographs and asks you to talk about them for one minute. The examiner then asks your partner a question about your photographs and your partner responds briefly.

Then the examiner gives your partner two different photographs. Your partner talks about these photographs for one minute. This time the examiner asks you a question about your partner's photographs and you respond briefly.

Part 3 (4 minutes)

The examiner asks you and your partner to talk together. You may be asked to solve a problem or try to come to a decision about something. For example, you might be asked to decide the best way to use some rooms in a language school. The examiner gives you some text to help you but does not join in the conversation.

Part 4 (4 minutes)

The examiner asks some further questions, which leads to a more general discussion of what you have talked about in Part 3. You may comment on your partner's answers if you wish.

Frames for the Speaking test

Test 1

Note: In the examination, there will be both an assessor and an interlocutor in the room. The visual material for **Test 1** appears on pages C1 and C2 (Part 2), and C3 (Part 3).

Part 1 2 minutes (3 minutes for groups of three)

Interlocutor: Good morning/afternoon/evening. My name is .... and this is my colleague ....
And your names are?
Can I have your mark sheets, please?
Thank you.

- Where are you from, *(Candidate A)*?
- And you, *(Candidate B)*?

First, we'd like to know something about you.

Select one or more questions from any of the following categories, as appropriate.

Family and friends
- Who are you most like in your family? (In what ways are you similar?)
- Do you go on holiday with your family? (Why? / Why not?)
- Have you done anything interesting with your friends recently? (What did you do with them?)
- Tell me about a really good friend of yours. (Do you share the same interests?)

Your interests
- Is there a sport or hobby you enjoy doing? (What do you do?) (Why do you like it?)
- If you could learn a new skill, what would you choose to do? (Why?)
- Do you like reading? (What do you read?) (Why do you like it?)
- Have you seen a good film recently? (Tell me about it.)

Future plans
- Have you got any plans for this weekend? (What are you going to do?)
- Are you going to go on holiday this year? (Where are you going to go?)
- Is there anything you'd like to study in the future? (Why?)
- Which country would you most like to visit in the future? (Do you think you'll go there one day?) (Why? / Why not?)

Part 2 4 minutes (6 minutes for groups of three)

Football games
Travelling

Interlocutor:	In this part of the test, I'm going to give each of you two photographs. I'd like you to talk about your photographs on your own for about a minute, and also to answer a question about your partner's photographs.
	(Candidate A), it's your turn first. Here are your photographs. They show people enjoying different football games.
	Indicate the pictures on page C1 to the candidates.
	I'd like you to compare the photographs, and say what you think the people are enjoying about these football games.
	All right?
Candidate A:	*[1 minute.]*
	Thank you.
Interlocutor:	*(Candidate B)*, do you enjoy watching football games? ..... (Why? / Why not?)
Candidate B:	*[Approximately 30 seconds.]*
Interlocutor:	Thank you.
	Now, *(Candidate B)*, here are your photographs. They show people travelling in different ways.
	Indicate the pictures on page C2 to the candidates.
	I'd like you to compare the photographs, and say what might be good or bad for the people about travelling in these ways.
	All right?
Candidate B:	*[1 minute.]*
Interlocutor:	Thank you.
	(Candidate A), do you prefer travelling by car or train? ..... (Why?)
Candidate A:	*[Approximately 30 seconds.]*
Interlocutor:	Thank you.

Parts 3 and 4   7 minutes (9 minutes for groups of three)

Part 3

The best way to buy

Interlocutor:	Now, I'd like you to talk about something together for about two minutes *(3 minutes for groups of three).*
	I'd like you to imagine that a teacher has asked her students to discuss whether it's better to buy things in shops or online. Here are some ideas the students have had and a question for you to discuss. First you have some time to look at the task.
	Indicate the text on page C3 to the candidates. Allow 15 seconds.
	Now, talk to each other about whether you think it's better to buy things in shops or online.
Candidates:	*[2 minutes (3 minutes for groups of three).]*
Interlocutor:	Thank you. Now you have about a minute to decide which of these things is most important to think about when you're buying something expensive.
Candidates:	*[1 minute (for pairs and groups of three).]*
Interlocutor:	Thank you.

Part 4

Interlocutor: *Use the following questions, in order, as appropriate:*

- Some people say there will be no need for shops in the future because we'll buy everything online.

- Do you think it's true that we buy a lot of things we don't really need these days? (Why? / Why not?)

> *Select any of the following prompts, as appropriate:*
> - What do you think?
> - Do you agree?
> - And you?

- Do you think that out of town shopping centres are a good idea?

- Is it better to go shopping with friends or alone?

- Some people say that shopping is a leisure activity nowadays. What do you think?

- Do you think that advertising encourages people to spend too much money? (Why? / Why not?)

Thank you. That is the end of the test.

Test 2

Note: In the examination, there will be both an assessor and an interlocutor in the room. The visual material for **Test 2** appears on pages C4 and C5 (Part 2), and C6 (Part 3).

Part 1 2 minutes (3 minutes for groups of three)

Interlocutor: Good morning/afternoon/evening. My name is ………… and this is my colleague ………… .
And your names are?
Can I have your mark sheets, please?
Thank you.

- Where are you from, *(Candidate A)*?
- And you, *(Candidate B)*?

First, we'd like to know something about you.

Select one or more questions from any of the following categories, as appropriate.

Family and friends
- Who are you most like in your family? (In what ways are you similar?)
- Do you go on holiday with your family? (Why? / Why not?)
- Have you done anything interesting with your friends recently? (What did you do with them?)
- Tell me about a really good friend of yours. (Do you share the same interests?)

Your interests
- Is there a sport or hobby you enjoy doing? (What do you do?) (Why do you like it?)
- If you could learn a new skill, what would you choose to do? (Why?)
- Do you like reading? (What do you read?) (Why do you like it?)
- Have you seen a good film recently? (Tell me about it.)

Future plans
- Have you got any plans for this weekend? (What are you going to do?)
- Are you going to go on holiday this year? (Where are you going to go?)
- Is there anything you'd like to study in the future? (Why?)
- Which country would you most like to visit in the future? (Do you think you'll go there one day?) (Why? / Why not?)

Part 2 4 minutes (6 minutes for groups of three)

Taking photographs
Different jobs

Interlocutor:	In this part of the test, I'm going to give each of you two photographs. I'd like you to talk about your photographs on your own for about a minute, and also to answer a question about your partner's photographs.
	(Candidate A), it's your turn first. Here are your photographs. They show people taking photographs in these situations.
	Indicate the pictures on page C4 to the candidates.
	I'd like you to compare the photographs, and say why you think the people are taking photographs in these situations.
	All right?
Candidate A:	*[1 minute.]*
Interlocutor:	Thank you.
	(Candidate B), Do you like taking photographs when you go on holiday? ..... (Why? / Why not?)
Candidate B:	*[Approximately 30 seconds.]*
Interlocutor:	Thank you.
	Now, *(Candidate B)*, here are your photographs. They show people doing different jobs.
	Indicate the pictures on page C5 to the candidates.
	I'd like you to compare the photographs, and say what might be difficult for the people about doing these jobs.
	All right?
Candidate B:	*[1 minute.]*
Interlocutor:	Thank you.
	(Candidate A), Which of these jobs would you prefer to do? ..... (Why?)
Candidate A:	*[Approximately 30 seconds.]*
Interlocutor:	Thank you.

Parts 3 and 4   7 minutes (9 minutes for groups of three)

Part 3

Television

Interlocutor:	Now, I'd like you to talk about something together for about two minutes *(3 minutes for groups of three)*.
	I'd like you to imagine that some students are doing a project about the influence of television on young people's lives. Here are some ideas they have had for the project and a question for you to discuss. First you have some time to look at the task.
	Indicate the text on page C6 to the candidates. Allow 15 seconds.
	Now, talk to each other about whether you think television has a good or a bad influence on young people's lives.
Candidates:	*[2 minutes (3 minutes for groups of three).]*
Interlocutor:	Thank you. Now you have about a minute to decide what is the best thing about television.
Candidates:	*[1 minute (for pairs and groups of three).]*
Interlocutor:	Thank you.

Part 4

Interlocutor: *Use the following questions, in order, as appropriate:*

- Is watching TV the best way for people to spend their free time? (Why? / Why not?)

- What kind of TV programmes do you like best? (Why?)

- Some people have more than one television in their home. Do you think this is a good idea? (Why / Why not?)

> *Select any of the following prompts, as appropriate:*
> - What do you think?
> - Do you agree?
> - And you?

- Do you think children generally watch too much television in (candidate's country)? (Why / Why not?)

- Is television the best way of following the news in the world? (Why? / Why not?)

- Do you think watching TV is a good way to learn a language? (Why / Why not?)

Thank you. That is the end of the test.

Test 3

Note: In the examination, there will be both an assessor and an interlocutor in the room. The visual material for **Test 3** appears on pages C7 and C8 (Part 2), and C9 (Part 3).

Part 1   2 minutes (3 minutes for groups of three)

Interlocutor: Good morning/afternoon/evening. My name is ………… and this is my colleague ………… .
And your names are?
Can I have your mark sheets, please?
Thank you.

- Where are you from, *(Candidate A)*?
- And you, *(Candidate B)*?

First we'd like to know something about you.

Select one or more questions from any of the following categories, as appropriate.

Family and friends
- Who are you most like in your family? (In what ways are you similar?)
- Do you go on holiday with your family? (Why? / Why not?)
- Have you done anything interesting with your friends recently? (What did you do with them?)
- Tell me about a really good friend of yours. (Do you share the same interests?)

Your interests
- Is there a sport or hobby you enjoy doing? (What do you do?) (Why do you like it?)
- If you could learn a new skill, what would you choose to do? (Why?)
- Do you like reading? (What do you read?) (Why do you like it?)
- Have you seen a good film recently? (Tell me about it.)

Future plans
- Have you got any plans for this weekend? (What are you going to do?)
- Are you going to go on holiday this year? (Where are you going to go?)
- Is there anything you'd like to study in the future? (Why?)
- Which country would you most like to visit in the future? (Do you think you'll go there one day?) (Why? / Why not?)

Part 2   4 minutes (6 minutes for groups of three)

In the evening
Family time

Interlocutor:	In this part of the test, I'm going to give each of you two photographs. I'd like you to talk about your photographs on your own for about a minute, and also to answer a question about your partner's photographs.
	(Candidate A), it's your turn first. Here are your photographs. They show people doing different things in the evening.
	Indicate the pictures on page C7 to the candidates.
	I'd like you to compare the photographs, and say what the people are enjoying about doing these things in the evening.
	All right?
Candidate A:	*[1 minute.]*
Interlocutor:	Thank you.
	(Candidate B), which of these things would you prefer to do in the evening? ..... (Why?)
Candidate B:	*[Approximately 30 seconds.]*
Interlocutor:	Thank you.
	Now, *(Candidate B)*, here are your photographs. They show families doing different things together in their free time.
	Indicate the pictures on page C8 to the candidates.
	I'd like you to compare the photographs, and say why the families have decided to do these things together in their free time.
	All right?
Candidate B:	*[1 minute.]*
Interlocutor:	Thank you.
	(Candidate A), which of these things would you prefer to do with your family? ..... (Why?)
Candidate A:	*[Approximately 30 seconds.]*
Interlocutor:	Thank you.

Parts 3 and 4   7 minutes (9 minutes for groups of three)

Part 3

Improving life

Interlocutor:	Now, I'd like you to talk about something together for about two minutes *(3 minutes for groups of three)*.
	Here are some ways that governments could improve life for people living in cities and a question for you to discuss. First you have some time to look at the task.
	Indicate the text on page C9 to the candidates. Allow 15 seconds.
	Now, talk to each other about whether these are good ways to improve life for people living in cities.
Candidates:	*[2 minutes (3 minutes for groups of three).]*
Interlocutor:	Thank you. Now you have about a minute to decide which of these things would have the greatest long-term benefit for people living in cities.
Candidates:	*[1 minute (for pairs and groups of three).]*
Interlocutor:	Thank you.

Part 4

Interlocutor: *Use the following questions, in order, as appropriate:*

- What's good about living in cities in (candidate's country)? (Why?)
- Which is the best city for people to visit in (candidate's country)? (Why?)
- If you could choose to visit a city you've never been to, which one would you choose? (Why?)
- Would you prefer to live in a modern city or a city with lots of history? (Why?)
- Are there advantages to living in a small town rather than in a big city?
- Do you think it is better for children to grow up in the city or in the countryside? (Why?)

> *Select any of the following prompts, as appropriate:*
>
> - What do you think?
> - Do you agree?
> - And you?

Thank you. That is the end of the test.

Test 4

Note: In the examination, there will be both an assessor and an interlocutor in the room. The visual material for **Test 4** appears on pages C10 and C11 (Part 2), and C12 (Part 3).

Part 1   2 minutes (3 minutes for groups of three)

Interlocutor: Good morning/afternoon/evening. My name is .... and this is my colleague ....
And your names are?
Can I have your mark sheets, please?
Thank you.

- Where are you from, *(Candidate A)*?
- And you, *(Candidate B)*?

First we'd like to know something about you.

Select one or more questions from any of the following categories, as appropriate.

Family and friends
- Who are you most like in your family? (In what ways are you similar?)
- Do you go on holiday with your family? (Why? / Why not?)
- Have you done anything interesting with your friends recently? (What did you do with them?)
- Tell me about a really good friend of yours. (Do you share the same interests?)

Your interests
- Is there a sport or hobby you enjoy doing? (What do you do?) (Why do you like it?)
- If you could learn a new skill, what would you choose to do? (Why?)
- Do you like reading? (What do you read?) (Why do you like it?)
- Have you seen a good film recently? (Tell me about it.)

Future plans
- Have you got any plans for this weekend? (What are you going to do?)
- Are you going to go on holiday this year? (Where are you going to go?)
- Is there anything you'd like to study in the future? (Why?)
- Which country would you most like to visit in the future? (Do you think you'll go there one day?) (Why? / Why not?)

Part 2 4 minutes (6 minutes for groups of three)

In the city
A special day

Interlocutor:	In this part of the test, I'm going to give each of you two photographs. I'd like you to talk about your photographs on your own for about a minute, and also to answer a question about your partner's photographs.
	(Candidate A), it's your turn first. Here are your photographs. They show people spending time in different places in a city.
	Indicate the pictures on page C10 to the candidates.
	I'd like you to compare the photographs, and say why the people have chosen to spend time in these different places in the city.
	All right?
Candidate A:	*[1 minute.]*
Interlocutor:	Thank you.
	(Candidate B), do you enjoy spending time in a city? ..... (Why? / Why not?)
Candidate B:	[Approximately 30 seconds.]
Interlocutor:	Thank you.
	Now, *(Candidate B)*, here are your photographs. They show people who are having a special day.
	Indicate the pictures on page C11 to the candidates.
	I'd like you to compare the photographs, and say what the people might enjoy about their special day.
	All right?
Candidate B:	*[1 minute.]*
Interlocutor:	Thank you.
	(Candidate A), do you enjoy celebrating with friends? ..... (Why? / Why not?)
Candidate A:	*[Approximately 30 seconds.]*
Interlocutor:	Thank you.

Parts 3 and 4   7 minutes (9 minutes for groups of three)

Part 3

**Important things
in life**

Interlocutor:	Now, I'd like you to talk about something together for about two minutes *(3 minutes for groups of three)*.
	Here are some things that many people think are important in their lives and a question for you to discuss. First you have some time to look at the task.
	Indicate the text on page C12 to the candidates. Allow 15 seconds.
	Now, talk to each other about why people think these things are important in their lives.
Candidates:	*[2 minutes (3 minutes for groups of three).]*
Interlocutor:	Thank you. Now you have about a minute to decide which two things become more important as people get older.
Candidates:	*[1 minute (for pairs and groups of three).]*
Interlocutor:	Thank you.

Part 4

Interlocutor: *Use the following questions, in order, as appropriate:*

- If you could change anything about your life, what would you change? (Why?)
- Many people say life's too busy these days. Why do you think they say this?
- Many people seem to want to become famous nowadays. Why do you think this is?
- Is it important to enjoy a job or do you think it's enough to be paid well? (Why?)
- How important is it to go on holiday every year? (Why? / Why not?)
- Some people say we don't spend enough time talking to each other these days. What do you think?

> *Select any of the following prompts, as appropriate:*
>
> - What do you think?
> - Do you agree?
> - And you?

Thank you. That is the end of the test.

Marks and results

Reading and Use of English

Candidates record their answers on a separate answer sheet. One mark is given for each correct answer in Parts 1, 2, 3 and 7. For Part 4, candidates are awarded a mark of 2, 1 or 0 for each question according to the accuracy of their response. Correct spelling is required in Parts 2, 3 and 4. Two marks are given for each correct answer in Parts 5 and 6. The final score is then weighted to 40 marks for the whole Reading and Use of English paper.

Writing

Examiners look at four aspects of your writing: Content, Communicative Achievement, Organisation and Language.

- Content focuses on how well you have fulfilled the task, in other words if you have done what you were asked to do.
- Communicative Achievement focuses on how appropriate the writing is for the letter or story and whether you have used the appropriate register.
- Organisation focuses on the way you put the piece of writing together, in other words if it is logical and ordered, and the punctuation is correct.
- Language focuses on your vocabulary and grammar. This includes the range of language as well as how accurate it is.

For each of the subscales, the examiner gives a maximum of 5 marks. Examiners use the following assessment scale:

B2	Content	Communicative Achievement	Organisation	Language
5	All content is relevant to the task. Target reader is fully informed.	Uses the conventions of the communicative task effectively to hold the target reader's attention and communicate straightforward and complex ideas, as appropriate.	Text is well organised and coherent, using a variety of cohesive devices and organisational patterns to generally good effect.	Uses a range of vocabulary, including less common lexis, appropriately. Uses a range of simple and complex grammatical forms with control and flexibility. Occasional errors may be present but do not impede communication.
4	*Performance shares features of Bands 3 and 5.*			

3	Minor irrelevances and/or omissions may be present. Target reader is on the whole informed.	Uses the conventions of the communicative task to hold the target reader's attention and communicate straightforward ideas.	Text is generally well organised and coherent, using a variety of linking words and cohesive devices.	Uses a range of everyday vocabulary appropriately, with occasional inappropriate use of less common lexis. Uses a range of simple and some complex grammatical forms with a good degree of control. Errors do not impede communication.
2	*Performance shares features of Bands 1 and 3.*			
1	Irrelevances and misinterpretation of task may be present. Target reader is minimally informed.	Uses the conventions of the communicative task in generally appropriate ways to communicate straightforward ideas.	Text is connected and coherent, using basic linking words and a limited number of cohesive devices.	Uses everyday vocabulary generally appropriately, while occasionally overusing certain lexis. Uses simple grammatical forms with a good degree of control. While errors are noticeable, meaning can still be determined.
0	Content is totally irrelevant. Target reader is not informed.	*Performance below Band 1.*		

Length of responses

Make sure you write the correct number of words. Responses which are too short may not have an adequate range of language and may not provide all the information that is required. Responses which are too long may contain irrelevant content and have a negative effect on the reader.

Varieties of English

You are expected to use a particular variety of English with some degree of consistency in areas such as spelling, and not for example switch from using a British spelling of a word to an American spelling of the same word.

Writing sample answers and examiner's comments.

The following pieces of writing have been selected from students' answers. The samples relate to tasks in Tests 1–4. Explanatory notes have been added to show how the bands have been arrived at.

Sample A (Test 1, Question 1 – Essay)

I agree life is better today than it was 100 years ago because of the development of technology and improvement of different condicions I will divid it into three parts to support my agreement.

First, in terms of health, because of the development on medicine and research about different diseases and virus, now people could control some diseases. Futhermore, doctors put their emphasize on researching how to cure some cancers. Therefore, people could lie longer than before. In addition, if people got sick, it would be easier than before to see the doctor and cure the sickness.

Second, nowadays, there are variety of entertainment than before especially the help of computers and internet. For example, people could surf on the internet to play games, download music, or watch movies. Moreoever, because of new technology in filming, people could just go to the cinemas and enjoy the fancy movies with great sounds and pictures even three digital movies.

Finally, transportation nowadays is more convenient than before. Before it took more time to travel from one place to another places. However, it became easier because of the invention of planes, high rapid trains and undergrounds. People travel by planes from countries to countries and enjoy different cultures and scenery.

In conclusion, life is better today in terms of health, entertainment and transportation.

Scales	Mark	Commentary
Content	5	All content is relevant to the task and the target reader is fully informed. The two points in the question are discussed and a third idea is added which is about transport.
Communicative Achievement	3	The conventions of essay writing are used to communicate straightforward ideas. The main points are explained and developed in an appropriate tone, which holds the target reader's attention.
Organisation	4	The text is well organised and coherent and makes use of a variety of suitable cohesive devices to develop the main points and connect the ideas throughout the text. The paragraphing works well as each one deals with a separate idea.
Language	4	There is a range of vocabulary which is used well *(in terms of health; cure some cancers; surf on the internet; the invention of)* and a range of simple and some complex grammatical forms is used with a good degree of control. There are some errors with less common lexis, but these do not impede communication.

Sample B (Test 1, Question 2 – Review)

I recently saw an amazing documentary which is called "Surprise". That sounds quite strange, but this great documentary is about animals. It is named "SURPRISE" because can you find out things that you don't really expect and so you will be surprised. For instance you can find out why elephants can't jump or why have got zebras stripes.

There are also another useful informations, things such as food, sleeping, how long do they leave and so on. However in my opinion the best are informations which you don't expect.

Each documentary is about different animal, because it depens on people what they would like to see because there is still phone numbers during the documentary, so people can phone and say what animal they are interesting in.

This documentary is good choice for all generations, because they can just relax during it and develop their skills about animals. Other advantage is that there aren't mrders, violence or burglars. There is only beautiful countryside, an interesting places and cute animals.

I could recommend this documentary to all people. It is worth it.

Scales	Mark	Commentary
Content	5	All content is relevant to the task and the target reader would be fully informed. We learn about the subject of the documentary, animals, and what was learned from it.
Communicative Achievement	3	The conventions of the communicative task are used to communicate straightforward ideas. The review describes the topic of the documentary and recommends who would find it interesting using an appropriate register which holds the reader's attention.
Organisation	3	The text is generally well organised and coherent. The documentary is introduced and the details of the programme are developed logically, using a variety of linking words and cohesive devices to connect the ideas through the text.
Language	2	There is a range of everyday vocabulary which is used appropriately, despite a number of spelling mistakes. There is a range of simple grammatical forms used with a good degree of control, but errors occur when more complex structures are attempted. Errors are noticeable, but they do not impede communication.

Sample C (Test 2, Question 3 – Article)

I think it was a year ago. Me, my friends, open air, mud and whole weekend spent listening to live concerts at Woodstock. It was a great experience for us. We've been there all alone, sleeping in a common tent, making food for each other. Nobody really cared about the time or school. It could be the only one chance in a lifetime. Me and my friends took part in mud-fight, took some amazing photos (even of us with the leader of our favourite band) and join one of the best parts of a concerts called "pogo".

This was a two-day event, and I will never forget that moment, when the leader of a band throw a guitar pick into the croud and … I caught it! It was dark, and a little lait used, but totally best thing from that day.

When last band ended the show, we watched the fireworks display and started to pack our things.

But there weren't only good moments. I mean: coming home, and leaving this place behind, was the worst thing ever.

Scales	Mark	Commentary
Content	5	All content is relevant to the task and the target reader would be fully informed. A weekend at a music festival is described and there are details about what happened there.
Communicative Achievement	5	The conventions of writing an article are used effectively to communicate both straightforward and some more complex ideas, for example the final sentence. The tone is engaging, suitable for a wide audience and the target reader's attention would be held throughout.
Organisation	4	The text is well organised and coherent and the events are described in sequential order, which is an appropriate organisational pattern for this article. The first two paragraphs show some good features of internal cohesion, which is in contrast to the final two paragraphs which are at sentence level.
Language	4	There is a range of vocabulary used appropriately, including some less common lexis which is specific to the topic. There is a range of simple and some more complex grammatical forms used with control. Errors occur generally when more ambitious language is attempted, or with spelling.

Sample D (Test 2, Question 4 – Email)

> *Hello Kim,*
>
> *It's my pleasure to let you staying at my place. You know I'm here for everything you may need, and until I come back from holiday, I won't need it anyway.*
>
> *To get the keys, ask to Manuel, my next door neighbour. I asked him to keep the keys before I left, so they were somewhere safe. He is a good and reliable friend. The blue key is for the main entrance of the building, and the other one is for the flat.*
>
> *Be specially careful with the heating, because it doesn't work properly, and sometimes it turns to over heat the place. Just don't pull the leaver too much, more or less over the middle.*
>
> *To buy food you can go to the grocery shop which is two blocks from the flat, going south. There you may find whatever you need, and if you say you know me and are living in my place now, I'm sure they will treat you very well.*
>
> *If you need something, please call me.*
>
> *See you.*

Scales	Mark	Commentary
Content	5	All content is relevant to the task and the target reader would be fully informed. The reader would know where the keys are, what problems to look out for and where to go shopping.
Communicative Achievement	5	The conventions of writing an informal email are used effectively. There is a friendly, natural tone used throughout; straightforward advice is given and suggestions are clearly made, which would make the stay in the flat easier.
Organisation	5	The text is well organised and coherent, dealing with each point in the question in turn and explaining each one clearly. The text uses a variety of cohesive devices to link the ideas across paragraphs and sentences and there are some organisational patterns used to generally good effect, for example the parallel opening phrases of the second and fourth paragraphs.
Language	4	There is a range of suitable, natural vocabulary used appropriately. There is a range of simple and complex grammatical forms used with control and although there are a few errors, *(let you staying)*, these do not impede communication.

Sample E (Test 3, Question 3 – Article)

> Happiness. Is just a common word but a word so often used in our daily life. Appears in every book or movie and for many of us stays the mein factor to have a valuable life. In fact, it is the feeling that everybody tries to get.
>
> I have been thinking it many times so far and even if so often I had a chance to get through and to know what it really means, it still slides away a little bit while taking the risk to describe it in words.
>
> The state of mind while being happy is one of the most wonderful moments in my life and even it naturally comes itself in the most unexpected moments, it reminds to rule beneath any other need. It is like a task to done, but sometimes it's just like a fresh wind, never tamed. It's a source of human's beauty, because people who feel it are able to give to the world more.
>
> Happiness to me is the possibility to be around the people I care about. It is hidden in landscapes from the childhood, which are changing with years but while on refreshing them by spending some time surrounded by nature, memories bring it back to life.
>
> When I ask myself why some simple things make me happy and why exactly them, I can't find any logical answer. Although when it comes I know it really exists.

Scales	Mark	Commentary
Content	5	All content is relevant and the target reader would be fully informed. The task has been approached from a slightly abstract viewpoint, but the points in the question have all been addressed.
Communicative Achievement	4	The conventions of the communicative task have been used to communicate some complex, abstract ideas, in an appropriate format and register which holds the attention of the target reader. Sometimes the language does not express the more complex ideas completely effectively, but it is an ambitious attempt, and the more straightforward ideas are communicated well.
Organisation	3	The text is generally well organised into paragraphs, although the abstract ideas are not always connected cohesively between the paragraphs. However, there is an overall coherence to the text and linking words and cohesive devices are used to connect ideas within and across sentences.
Language	4	There is a range of vocabulary and some phrases are used to very good effect *(but sometimes it's just like a fresh wind, never tamed)*. However, grammatical forms and some more complex phrases are not always used with full control.

Sample F (Test 3, Question 4 – Letter)

> Dear Sir or Madam,
>
> I am writing to apply for the Travel Competition that appeared on the advertisement of the Local English Language newspaper last week. I would like to have the opportunity to participate in the travel competition as a member of your team.
>
> I am very interested in going on the trip because I am young, healthy and I like doing adventure sports such as climbing, skiing, paragliding, canoeing… Moreover, I like sharing this kind of experiences with other people because I enjoy doing task group.
>
> In this moment, I am in good conditions phisically and psicologically because I have been living in the jungle; in the Amazon, in hard conditions for two months as a member of 'Supervivientes' in a T.V. programme of Channel 5 in Spain. We had to survive without food and water and I learnt to fish and hunt. It was a fantastic experience I did great friends.
>
> I'm very glad if I could participate on a Round World trip as you mention.
>
> I look forward to receiving your reply as soon as possible.
>
> Yours faithfully

Scales	Mark	Commentary
Content	5	All content is relevant to the task and the target reader would be fully informed. The reader would know where the keys are, what problems to look out for and where to go shopping.
Communicative Achievement	4	The conventions of formal letter writing have been used effectively. The tone is formal and polite and some key phrases for a letter of application have been used (*I am writing to apply for; I look forward to receiving your reply as soon as possible*). Straightforward ideas are expressed clearly and the target reader's attention would be held.
Organisation	2	The text is generally well organised and coherent. There is good use of paragraphs and the sentences are connected with basic linking words and a limited number of cohesive devices.
Language	3	Everyday vocabulary is used appropriately and there is a range of simple and some more complex grammatical forms used with a good degree of control (*I have been living in the jungle in the Amazon; we had to survive without food and water*). There are a few errors, but these do not impede communication (*I did great friends; I am in good conditions phisically*).

Sample G (Test 4, Question 1 – Essay)

> I agree it is vital to protect our environment as it is own habitant and it is vital for our well-being. Protecting the environment goes hand in hand with saving or protecting the endangered species.
>
> We should not let the populations of tigers, pandas or koalas go extinct. Since it is mostly our fault that the numbers of certain kinds of animals, we need to take the responsibility and try to save them. Animals being hunted for their fur, claws, horns or even meat is a terrifying image that really concerns me.
>
> I think all of us have at least once need a book or watched a movie showing tigers or lions as mighty creatures strong, powerful, beautiful, as children we were amazed by their appearance and wanted to be as brave, as strong or as big as them. I do not want to live to the moment when I will have to explain to my children that these magnificent creatures do not exist anymore because of us, humans.
>
> I am a fan of the PETA organisation and I would always vote for banning selling clothing and products made of anything from the animals. We also have to spread the information about this issue around and raise the public awareness. I believe that no changes can happen unless the majority of us does not make the first step.

Scales	Mark	Commentary
Content	5	All the content is relevant and the target reader would be fully informed. The two points in the question are developed and a third is discussed which is about the use of products derived from animals and raising public awareness of the issue.
Communicative Achievement	5	The conventions of essay writing have been used effectively to discuss the issues in an informed way. The tone of the essay is consistently formal and both straightforward and complex ideas are presented and developed in a way which holds the target reader's attention throughout.
Organisation	4	The essay is well organised and coherent, with particularly good use of paragraphs which focus on and develop one aspect of the essay topic. There is a variety of linking words and cohesive devices used to connect the ideas through the text.
Language	3	Everyday vocabulary is used appropriately, but there are errors with word order when expressing more complex ideas (*as it is own habitant; live to the moment; the numbers of certain kinds of animals*). There is a range of simple and some more complex grammatical forms used with a good degree of control. Errors do not impede.

Sample H (Test 4, Question 4 – Report)

<u>Introduction</u>

A good place that my college would recommend to the group of English students to visit is Port Aventura.

<u>The attraction:</u>

Port Aventura is a place where all types of people can have fun and enjoy at the same time. It as a lot of roller coasters for the ones that want an exciting and adventurous experience and for the people that prefers quite places they have some theatres and different shows at all time, or even it's worth for the people that just want to see the place and have a walk around there. Moreover, you can find really good places to eat and some shops if you have money to spend.

<u>Why they would enjoy it:</u>

I think that students would enjoy visiting it because after a long term with exams, homework and classes, it is very interesting for them to have a day enjoying with rollercoasters and spending time with their friends and schoolmates. In addition, they will like it because are teenagers and Port Aventura is the perfect place to spend a different day doing something fun.

<u>Conclusion</u>

In conclusion, I think that Port Aventura it is a good place to go for the students because it will improve the relations with their schoolmates and it is the perfect place to spend a day having fun.

Scales	Mark	Commentary
Content	5	All content is relevant and the target reader would be fully informed. The report describes a location, explains what can be done there and why it would be suitable for a group of students.
Communicative Achievement	4	The report has been written using the conventions of the genre, for example headings and a concluding recommendation. The tone is objective and formal throughout. The report states straightforward facts and comments on them in a way which would effectively hold the reader's attention.
Organisation	4	The report is well organised and coherent, with particularly good use of headings which separate the main points. The text within the paragraphs is connected with a variety of linking words and cohesive devices.
Language	4	There is a range of task specific vocabulary used appropriately (*a long term with exams; improve the relations*). A range of simple and some more complex grammatical structures are used with control. There are some errors, (*that prefers quite; it's worth for*) but these do not impede.

Listening

One mark is given for each correct answer. The total is weighted to give a mark out of 40 for the paper. In **Part 2**, minor spelling errors are allowed, provided that the candidate's intention is clear.

For security reasons, several versions of the Listening paper are used at each administration of the examination. Before grading, the performance of the candidates in each of the versions is compared and marks adjusted to compensate for any imbalance in levels of difficulty.

Speaking

Throughout the test candidates are assessed on their own individual performance and not in relation to the other candidate. They are assessed on their language skills, not on their personality, intelligence or knowledge of the world. Candidates must, however, be prepared to develop the conversation and respond to the tasks in an appropriate way.

Candidates are awarded marks by two examiners: the assessor and the interlocutor. The assessor awards marks by applying performance descriptors from the Analytical Assessment scales for the following criteria:

Grammar and Vocabulary
This refers to the accurate use of grammatical forms and appropriate use of vocabulary. It also includes the range of language.

Discourse Management
This refers to the extent, relevance and coherence of each candidate's contributions. Candidates should be able to construct clear stretches of speech which are easy to follow. The length of their contributions should be appropriate to the task, and what they say should be related to the topic and the conversation in general.

Pronunciation
This refers to the intelligibility of contributions at word and sentence levels. Candidates should be able to produce utterances that can easily be understood, and which show control of intonation, stress and individual sounds.

Interactive Communication
This refers to the ability to use language to achieve meaningful communication. Candidates should be able to initiate and respond appropriately according to the task and conversation, and also to use interactive strategies to maintain and develop the communication whilst negotiating towards an outcome.

B2	Grammar and Vocabulary	Discourse Management	Pronunciation	Interactive Communication
5	• Shows a good degree of control of a range of simple and some complex grammatical forms. • Uses a range of appropriate vocabulary to give and exchange views on a wide range of familiar topics.	• Produces extended stretches of language with very little hesitation. • Contributions are relevant and there is a clear organisation of ideas. • Uses a range of cohesive devices and discourse markers.	• Is intelligible. • Intonation is appropriate. • Sentence and word stress is accurately placed. • Individual sounds are articulated clearly.	• Initiates and responds appropriately, linking contributions to those of other speakers. • Maintains and develops the interaction and negotiates towards an outcome.
4	*Performance shares features of Bands 3 and 5.*			
3	• Shows a good degree of control of simple grammatical forms, and attempts some complex grammatical forms. • Uses a range of appropriate vocabulary to give and exchange views on a range of familiar topics.	• Produces extended stretches of language despite some hesitation. • Contributions are relevant and there is very little repetition. • Uses a range of cohesive devices.	• Is intelligible. • Intonation is generally appropriate. • Sentence and word stress is generally accurately placed. • Individual sounds are generally articulated clearly.	• Initiates and responds appropriately. • Maintains and develops the interaction and negotiates towards an outcome with very little support.
2	*Performance shares features of Bands 1 and 3.*			
1	• Shows a good degree of control of simple grammatical forms. • Uses a range of appropriate vocabulary when talking about everyday situations.	• Produces responses which are extended beyond short phrases, despite hesitation. • Contributions are mostly relevant, despite some repetition. • Uses basic cohesive devices.	• Is mostly intelligible, and has some control of phonological features at both utterance and word levels.	• Initiates and responds appropriately. • Keeps the interaction going with very little prompting and support.
0	*Performance below Band 1.*			

The interlocutor awards a mark for overall performance using a Global Achievement scale.

B2	Global Achievement
5	• Handles communication on a range of familiar topics, with very little hesitation. • Uses accurate and appropriate linguistic resources to express ideas and produce extended discourse that is generally coherent.
4	*Performance shares features of Bands 3 and 5.*
3	• Handles communication on familiar topics, despite some hesitation. • Organises extended discourse but occasionally produces utterances that lack coherence, and some inaccuracies and inappropriate usage occur.
2	*Performance shares features of Bands 1 and 3.*
1	• Handles communication in everyday situations, despite hesitation. • Constructs longer utterances but is not able to use complex language except in well-rehearsed utterances.
0	*Performance below Band 1.*

Assessment for *Cambridge English: First* is based on performance across all parts of the test, and is achieved by applying the relevant descriptors in the assessment scales.

Test 1 Key

Reading and Use of English (1 hour 15 minutes)

Part 1

1 A   2 C   3 A   4 B   5 C   6 D   7 B   8 D

Part 2

9 can/may   10 so   11 with   12 not/hardly/scarcely   13 and   14 have
15 where   16 if

Part 3

17 unknown   18 reference   19 popularity   20 marriage   21 fashionable
22 illnesses   23 labourers   24 energetic

Part 4

25 FEW programmes | were sold
26 INSTEAD of | taking/catching/getting
27 had/'d NEVER | broken
28 would | LOOK into/at
29 was/got postponed | BECAUSE it rained
30 to CARRY on | working

Part 5

31 B   32 D   33 D   34 B   35 A   36 C

Part 6

37 D   38 G   39 F   40 A   41 C   42 E

Part 7

43 C   44 C   45 A   46 B   47 A   48 C   49 B   50 D   51 B   52 D

Writing (1 hour 20 minutes)

Candidate responses are marked using the assessment scale on pages 107–108.

Listening (approximately 40 minutes)

Part 1

1 B   2 B   3 C   4 B   5 C   6 A   7 B   8 B

Part 2

9 geography
10 (street) markets
11 magazine
12 horses
13 winter
14 motor(-)bike
15 fishing
16 March
17 Images
18 farming

Part 3

19 E   20 H   21 B   22 G   23 D

Part 4

24 B   25 A   26 C   27 A   28 B   29 B   30 C

Transcript *This is the Cambridge English: First, Test One.*

I am going to give you the instructions for this test. I shall introduce each part of the test and give you time to look at the questions. At the start of each piece you will hear this sound:

tone

You will hear each piece twice.

Remember, while you are listening, write your answers on the question paper. You will have five minutes at the end of the test to copy your answers onto the separate answer sheet.

There will now be a pause. Please ask any questions now, because you must not speak during the test.

[pause]

Now open your question paper and look at Part One.

[pause]

PART 1   *You will hear people talking in eight different situations. For questions 1 to 8, choose the best answer (A, B or C).*

Question 1   *One.*
You hear a woman talking on her mobile phone about a missing piece of furniture.

[pause]

tone

I see, it wasn't in the van. But never mind, I'll call the removals company. It's OK, I'm sure it'll be fine, I just wonder what they've done with it. I mean it isn't something you can easily lose, is it? You'd think someone would've noticed almost straightaway. I'm sure it'll turn up very soon. So don't get too upset about it – it's just rather odd. And considering all the things that could have gone wrong, I think we've been fairly lucky really, don't you?

[pause]

tone

[The recording is repeated.]

[pause]

Question 2   *Two.*
You hear two students talking about their current course topic.

[pause]

tone

Woman: I think the lectures are really fascinating, don't you?
Man: Only if you're interested in that period of history. You'd think the lecture would have moved on to the next period by now. It's much more interesting.
Woman: But we needed extra time on it because it's such a complex area.
Man: Yeah, I can't make head nor tail of it!
Woman: We need to get to grips with it though or we won't be able to manage what's coming next.
Man: But is it really useful anyway?
Woman: Oh, come on. Let's get a coffee.

[pause]

tone

[The recording is repeated.]

[pause]

Question 3	*Three.* *You hear two business people talking about a contract.*

[pause]

tone

Man: Have you heard that the contract's been cancelled?

Woman: No, I had no idea! You must be really annoyed after all the work you put into it.

Man: Initially, I was, yes. I spent three weeks putting it all together and the company were really positive about it. But then I found out that they're in some financial difficulty so it's really unfortunate for them. We've worked with them for years.

Woman: It was a huge contract, wasn't it. What are you going to do now?

Man: Well, we've just had a very big order from one of our trusted clients so that's taken any pressure off.

[pause]

tone

[The recording is repeated.]

[pause]

Question 4	*Four.* *You hear an artist telling a friend about an art prize he's just won.*

[pause]

tone

Woman: You must be thrilled after the announcement that you've won such a famous art prize!

Man: Well, to be honest, I'm not quite sure how I feel yet! I'd always wondered about the idea of an art prize – I mean, it's not exactly a competition, so it seems strange. And you never quite know what the judges are looking for when they pick a winner.

Woman: Really?

Man: Well, yes. But actually, when I was on my own in the studio, I felt much more positive about it and even started dreaming about how my career would change now – not to mention what I'll do with the money!

Woman: Well, good luck!

[pause]

tone

[The recording is repeated.]

[pause]

Question 5

Five.
You overhear a woman talking to a friend on her mobile phone.

[pause]

tone

I don't mind when you come over, as long as it isn't too late – six thirty would be fine and give us time to have a really good chat. Is that OK? I have to get up early on Thursday morning, because I have to get the earlier flight. I'd booked myself on a ten o'clock one, but that's been cancelled. There's another one in the afternoon, but I'd miss the meeting if I took that one. It's a bit of a nuisance, but there you go. Anyway, it'll be great to see you!

[pause]

tone

[The recording is repeated.]

[pause]

Question 6

Six.
You hear a guitarist talking about his profession.

[pause]

tone

People ask me how to set up a band, but that's a matter of luck, there's no simple answer. Find people who want it as badly as you do, who can also be your best friends. I want to say something about the difficulty of learning to be a musician. It takes thousands of hours of practice, you have to be blessed with talent, you have to have day jobs until you finally make it, but if you have a passion for something, and you work hard enough, you'll get there. You'll soon find out which are the venues with the most enthusiastic fans.

[pause]

tone

[The recording is repeated.]

[pause]

Question 7

Seven.
You hear a woman talking to a sales assistant.

[pause]

tone

Assistant:	Hello, can I help you?
Woman:	Yes, I bought these trainers from your company online, and I really like them and everything, but they're a bit tight. I was wondering if you could give me a refund.
Assistant:	Sorry, I'm afraid we can't do that.
Woman:	Why not? It's obvious I haven't worn them and I've still got the receipt. Is it because I bought them online? Aren't you legally required to give a refund?
Assistant:	No, it's not that. These trainers don't come from here. Look at the receipt. It's got the wrong name on. Try next door.

[pause]

tone

[The recording is repeated.]

[pause]

Question 8   *Eight.*
You hear a woman talking about a radio chat show.

[pause]

tone

I love listening to The Clare Nolan show on Friday at eight o'clock. She has great guests and they often have a good time together on the show. Clare has a way of getting people to say things which come across as very funny. She doesn't come across as a celebrity, but more a normal person who is clever and tells us things we don't know in an enthusiastic and useful manner. She's good at doing that at the same time as making her guests feel involved. So many presenters nowadays seem to use their shows just to show off their own talents, but not Clare Nolan.

[pause]

tone

[The recording is repeated.]

[pause]

That is the end of Part One.

Now turn to Part Two.

[pause]

PART 2   *You will hear a photographer called Ian Gerrard talking about his career. For questions 9 to 18, complete the sentences with a word or short phrase.*

You now have forty-five seconds to look at Part Two.

[pause]

tone

Good evening, everyone. My name's Ian Gerrard and I'm a photographer. I'm here to tell you a bit about my career so far, and also about my new book.

I often get asked if I studied photography at university and people are sometimes surprised that I didn't. I wanted to, but my parents wouldn't let me, so I had to choose something else. I loved history but my marks weren't very good, but I was keen on geography too, so that is what I did in the end. I actually think it's made me a better photographer, and has given my work a broader context.

On my degree course, in my final year, we studied all aspects of the development of cities and we had to do a presentation. We could do what we wanted and it was really interesting the topics people chose. I chose street markets for mine but a friend did his on the growth of urban transport networks.

On graduation, I went to the USA. I knew I wanted to work as a photographer, so I'd sent pictures to news organisations and advertising agencies, hoping I might get something in a brochure, or even a newspaper! In fact, it was a magazine that noticed my pictures, and I worked for it for a year.

I learnt a huge amount, but what I really wanted to do was see the USA for myself. I needed a theme, something really American – maybe photographing diners or shopping malls around the country. Then I remembered all those westerns I'd seen and I just knew it had to be horses – I'd found what I wanted to focus on!

It was an amazing six months – I started off in the baking heat of summer on the east coast, and finished my journey up in the mountains. I get the most striking shots in the winter light, although I do love the warmth in summer photos.

Anyway, I came back to Britain at the beginning of spring and published my US photos in a small book. I earned just enough to finance my next trip – round the UK. I felt it was time I explored my own country. I'd done a lot of driving in the USA and I wanted a change from the car, so went by motorbike instead. I love train travel, but I wanted to get to more remote areas.

I wanted to explore the relationship between people and place. Interestingly, in the last few decades, many photographers from the UK haven't done much on fishing communities here, so that's what I did. They've tended to focus on family life in inner city communities instead.

The resulting photos I'm putting together for my new book. One thing I've learnt is that it takes ages to produce a book – almost as long, in fact, as it took me to travel around Britain and then develop all the photos I'd taken. I started my journey in August, and finished last month, in November. My book won't be in the shops until March, though there's an exhibition of my pictures touring the UK from January.

It's funny, I really wanted to call my book *Visions*, but apparently there's already one called that, so my publishers suggested the title *In Focus*, which I thought was horrible. In the end we settled for *Images*, which is OK.

Now I'm planning my next tour. I wasn't sure which theme to choose this time. I initially thought I'd look at lakes and mountains but then I saw a tractor in a field and I knew I'd do farming. I've decided to use a special camera to create very large photos, which I'm hoping to exhibit next year.

Well, if you have any questions ……. [fade]

[pause]

Now you will hear Part Two again.

tone

[pause]

[The recording is repeated.]

[pause]

That is the end of Part Two.

Now turn to Part Three.

[pause]

PART 3 *You will hear five short extracts in which people are talking about the benefits of learning another language. For questions 19 to 23, choose which benefit (A to H) each speaker has experienced. Use the letters only once. There are three extra letters which you do not need to use.*

You now have thirty seconds to look at Part Three.

[pause]

tone

Speaker 1

I know people from all around the world, because my job involves looking for global solutions to environmental problems. I get to go abroad a lot and I do think speaking or reading the language of a country has been a huge help when I've visited. Of course, I've friends who've been all over without speaking another language, and they've been able to make themselves understood. But I've usually found that when I'm somewhere I can speak the language, I worry less about the practical aspects of a journey and focus on enjoying what's going on around me. And that's what it's all about really.

[pause]

Speaker 2

Basically, it's pretty obvious: the better you can speak a language – or the more languages you know – the greater the number of people you can communicate with. In my case, I've formed close ties with a number of people from other countries. That's usually because we all appreciate the time and effort we've spent getting to know a different language and culture. I'm lucky because languages were well taught at my school. I wasn't actually considered to be particularly clever, but I was given a good start as far as other languages are concerned. I'm very grateful for that.

[pause]

Speaker 3

People often think I must be super-intelligent to be doing the course I'm doing but I don't think that's the case. I'm hoping to have a career in global finance, and the big advantage when I was applying for this college was the fact that I could speak several languages. That really helped me get in and I've met people from all over the world here. When I was a child, my parents travelled around a great deal. Luckily, I was a sociable child, so in every new country we lived in, I learnt the language quite quickly.

[pause]

Speaker 4

If you've ever travelled to a country where people speak a different language from your own, then you'll know that you can't just learn a list of words if you want to make yourself understood. The same idea is often expressed differently in other languages. So it's actually taught me a lot about my mother tongue. When you speak a foreign language, you have to actively think about what you want to say and how you want to say it. I find it helps if I think about the grammar in my native language first – something I'd never really thought about before. I certainly didn't when I was at school.

[pause]

Speaker 5

It's other people who have helped me learn languages, by letting me struggle on in their native tongue even when they knew mine far better! So I have a lot of kind and patient people to thank. I could never concentrate in language classes at school, but then I realised how important languages are these days. After all, in our globalised world, knowing more than your own language is extremely useful. I wouldn't already be at the level I am now professionally in my career if I didn't speak a few languages reasonably well. It's good to know all the travelling I did after leaving school wasn't wasted!

[pause]

Now you will hear Part Three again.

tone

[The recording is repeated.]

[pause]

That is the end of Part Three.

Now turn to Part Four.

[pause]

PART 4   *You will hear an interview with a woman called Patricia Jones, who is a naturalist. For questions 24 to 30, choose the best answer (A, B or C).*

You now have one minute to look at Part Four.

[pause]

tone

Interviewer: Patricia, this year marks the twentieth anniversary of the start of your elephant project in Africa. What are your feelings?

Patricia: Well, it's extraordinary to me to think that twenty years have passed, that I'm still working on the same projects and that hundreds of students who have volunteered with us have now got university teaching positions all over the world. That's probably had an impact on thousands of people by now, not just the foreign visitors coming to Africa, but locals as well.

Interviewer: How do you spend your time nowadays?

Patricia: Well, to begin with, my work was just concerned with learning about the behaviour of elephants in Africa. But then I realised that survival of the species depends on the actions of governments, big multi-nationals and ordinary people. So now I tend to focus more on getting people to realise the effect their actions have on wildlife and natural habitats. I try to demonstrate that by making a small change in the choices they make, for example in the products they buy, people can have a big effect on the wider world.

Interviewer: Do you think zoos have a part to play in conservation?

Patricia: Well, there are some old-fashioned zoos where the animals are kept in small cages for the entertainment of the public. The animals aren't able to express their natural behaviour and those zoos should definitely be shut down immediately. The best thing is for an animal to live in its natural environment, but we have this idealised view of freedom where their lives will be wonderful. The reality is that in so many places there are hunters. Sometimes we have to step in and offer a species protection, and that's where the new type of zoos come in.

Interviewer: In your new book, entitled *Animals and Their Habitats*, what message are you hoping to convey?

Patricia: The natural world is in real crisis, but there are extraordinary people all around the planet who are absolutely determined that endangered animal species or plants or ecosystems should be helped to restore themselves. I hope it'll be inspiring for young biologists and botanists at the outset of their careers to read about these people who have taken on these huge challenges.

Interviewer: Have children, do you think, lost that sense of connection to the natural world?

Patricia: Yes. We should be encouraging them to get back in touch with nature either by taking them into a natural environment or by bringing nature to the child. You know, research has shown that contact with the natural world is actually crucial for psychological growth. So many children have such little opportunity to experience nature and only do so second-hand from a TV screen.

Interviewer: What does your organisation called *In Touch* aim to do?

Patricia: Well, it's all youth driven, so it's young people discussing the problems they see around them and then between them choosing three projects to work on that they feel would make things better. One project is about people, one is about

	animals, and one is about the environment. So, in any group of young people, you get those passionate about animals, you get some who want to do community service for people and you have some who want to help the local environment.
Interviewer:	Do you think you still have a role to play?
Patricia:	Judging from the number of girls who write and say they want to follow in my footsteps, I think I do! But what I'd really like to do is stop people blaming science for everything. Many people think that it's scientists who are damaging the environment. I want people to see that they themselves are responsible too and that they can also be part of the solution by being conscious about the choices they make in their everyday lives. That's what I want to achieve.
Interviewer:	Many thanks Patricia … [fade]

[pause]

Now you will hear Part Four again.

tone

[The recording is repeated.]

[pause]

That is the end of Part Four.

There will now be a pause of five minutes for you to copy your answers onto the separate answer sheet. Be sure to follow the numbering of all the questions. I shall remind you when there is one minute left, so that you are sure to finish in time.

[Teacher, pause the recording here for five minutes. Remind students when they have one minute left.]

That is the end of the test. Please stop now. Your supervisor will now collect all the question papers and answer sheets.

Test 2 Key

Reading and Use of English (1 hour 15 minutes)

Part 1
1 B   2 D   3 D   4 A   5 D   6 B   7 A   8 C

Part 2
9 One   10 far   11 it   12 every/each   13 because   14 like
15 which/that   16 as

Part 3
17 unbelievable   18 considerably   19 limiting   20 minimise/minimize
21 identified   22 efficient   23 possibility   24 characteristics

Part 4
25 was | the FIRST time (that)
26 could NOT | have
27 has been | no INCREASE OR has not/hasn't been any/an INCREASE
28 is not/isn't BIG | enough to
29 (that) he would/could AVOID | spilling OR as to AVOID | spilling
30 PREVENTED me (from) / my | getting

Part 5
31 D   32 C   33 D   34 B   35 C   36 A

Part 6
37 F   38 C   39 D   40 A   41 G   42 B

Part 7
43 C   44 A   45 B   46 D   47 B   48 A   49 D   50 B   51 C   52 A

Writing (1 hour 20 minutes)

Candidate responses are marked using the assessment scale on pages 107–108.

Listening (approximately 40 minutes)

Part 1

1 B   2 C   3 A   4 B   5 C   6 B   7 B   8 C

Part 2

9 teacher   10 3,000 / three thousand   11 travel writer   12 airports   13 passengers
14 science   15 controls   16 monitor   17 report   18 night

Part 3

19 D   20 B   21 G   22 C   23 E

Part 4

24 C   25 B   26 B   27 A   28 C   29 B   30 A

Transcript   *This is the Cambridge English: First, Test Two.*

I am going to give you the instructions for this test. I shall introduce each part of the test and give you time to look at the questions. At the start of each piece you will hear this sound:

tone

You will hear each piece twice.

Remember, while you are listening, write your answers on the question paper. You will have five minutes at the end of the test to copy your answers onto the separate answer sheet.

There will now be a pause. Please ask any questions now, because you must not speak during the test.

[pause]

Now open your question paper and look at Part One.

[pause]

PART 1   *You will hear people talking in eight different situations. For questions 1 to 8, choose the best answer (A, B or C).*

Question 1   One.
You hear a man talking about how his business became successful.

[pause]

tone

I started this business with a really small budget. I tried to run it really economically, using the money I'd saved over the years and I chose to sell my products in quality stores for the first year before approaching the supermarkets. Then my business suddenly took off and I knew if I wanted to continue to grow, I really needed to make a series of TV advertisements and that required more money than I personally had. Someone my mother knew offered to help me out, which was really lucky because I'd tried applying to the bank for a loan but the interest rates were too high.

[pause]

tone

[The recording is repeated.]

[pause]

Question 2   *Two.*
You hear a woman talking about a journey.

[pause]

tone

Well I thought it was pretty uncomfortable, really. We had to be on board half an hour before we set off – I've no idea why – and then didn't stop at a service station for four hours. Four hours, can you imagine? We couldn't even get up to stretch our legs. We were just stuck in our seats, and when we did eventually stop, it was a rush to find a snack and a drink before we had to get on again. But it was cheap, and the new bridge means you don't have to take those awful ferries, which is definitely a bonus!

[pause]

tone

[The recording is repeated.]

[pause]

Question 3 *Three.*
You overhear a man talking to his wife on the phone.

[pause]

tone

It'll be great, you'll see! We won't just be stuck in one place, we'll be able to go on day trips wherever we want, and see all sorts of interesting sights. We won't be rushing to catch the bus to work every morning – we'll actually have time to sit down and have breakfast together – it seems a shame that we only have time to do things like that when we're away on holiday. Fancy having to leave the country to have a relaxed breakfast! I know it's expensive, but I definitely think it'll be worth it. And when you pass, you'll get the benefit too!

[pause]

tone

[The recording is repeated.]

[pause]

Question 4 *Four.*
You hear two students talking about their course.

[pause]

tone

Man: That was a good lecture, wasn't it?
Woman: Yeah, not bad – I just wish the course was a bit more challenging sometimes.
Man: Do you? I find it quite hard enough already, actually!
Woman: Well, at the beginning of term, I thought it was going to be great, you know, and looking into it all in more depth would be fascinating ... but now I'm not so sure.
Man: So do you think you might do something else instead next year?
Woman: No, I'll definitely carry on – I am learning and I need the qualification, even if it's just so I can go on to do something a bit more relevant later on!

[pause]

tone

[The recording is repeated.]

[pause]

Question 5 *Five.*
You hear a woman talking about roller derby, a hobby which involves speed racing on skates.

[pause]

tone

My roller derby skates are the most expensive footwear I've ever owned. It's a tough, physical game, and I think that's been the most astonishing thing for friends to understand, when I tell them which sport I've taken up. They're always amazed when they see me too, as our team races against another one around a track at incredible speed. It's thrilling – a great way of just leaving all my worries behind for a few hours. But of course body protection like a big helmet and knee pads are essential, so I admit I must be pretty unrecognisable like that – especially since in my daily life I look so ordinary!

[pause]

tone

[The recording is repeated.]

[pause]

Question 6   *Six.*
You hear part of a radio programme.

[pause]

tone

I'm sure it'll be popular, especially with sporty types. There's a lot of swimming gear on display – it's fascinating to see how different types of swimwear can affect a swimmer's performance. It actually made me want to get out there and do something active myself! You can book tickets online, and it's open seven days a week. And of course once you're in the building, there are all the permanent collections to look at too, if you want to. So whether you're like me and a bit of a couch potato, or fit and into exercise already, go and have a look!

[pause]

tone

[The recording is repeated.]

[pause]

Question 7   *Seven.*
You overhear two students discussing a reading project they did with young children.

[pause]

tone

Man:	So did you like working with the little kids, reading with them and everything? The books we chose for them from our library went down a storm, didn't they? Especially the bits we read out loud.
Woman:	Yeah, though I wondered if the really little ones could hear properly – it's such a big space. It was good fun, though …
Man:	Like when we started giving away the gifts we'd brought them.
Woman:	It's a pity the weather wasn't good – we should've been out in the sunshine. That room's meant to hold the whole school – about six hundred kids …
Man:	Well, at least we got out to play football with them in the break …

[pause]

tone

[The recording is repeated.]

[pause]

Question 8   *Eight.*
You hear an actor talking about the character she plays in a TV drama series.

[pause]

tone

Well, I enjoy playing her because she's so complex. She can be really sharp-tongued and gives brilliant one-liners. I wish I could do that! She's a clever lady but I wouldn't want to spend my time jetting all over the world like she does. I think it's really important to understand the character you're playing, you know, to try and get inside the character's head, so I've invented a whole backstory for her. I'm sure that at some point in the future she'll have a romance. Then you'd see a different side to her.

[pause]

tone

[The recording is repeated.]

[pause]

That is the end of Part One.

Now turn to Part Two.

[pause]

PART 2   *You will hear an interview with a woman called Gina Purvis, who is a pilot for a commercial airline. For questions 9 to18, complete the sentences with a word or short phrase.*

You now have forty-five seconds to look at Part Two.

[pause]

tone

Hello everyone. My name's Gina Purvis and I work as a pilot for a commercial airline. I'm going to tell you about my career. When I was about ten, I dreamt of being a flight attendant. Then the dream moved on to being a vet and working with animals, which actually I'd have hated because I hate seeing animals in pain. In fact, after school I went to train as a teacher and after I qualified I worked for a few years, but not with any great enthusiasm I must say. So how did I get started with flying?

Well, my mum bought me some flying lessons for a birthday present and I loved it from the start. I've been a commercial pilot for ten years now, and captain for the last five. The airline I work for demands that pilots have a minimum of three hundred flying hours experience initially, and to be eligible to become a captain, it's three thousand hours.

At the moment, I'm flying people to their holiday destinations around the Mediterranean. Some people ask me if my work interferes with my private life and friends outside work can struggle to understand why I'm not available on Friday or Saturday nights. It really helps that I'm married to a travel writer, who understands the air industry. Other pilots, whose partners are bank managers and things like that, find it hard. And we don't have any children so it all works, somehow.

Now, before I take off, I have to consult the 'Notices to Pilots', as they're called. That gives me news of airports having any problems. For example, one of the runways at London Gatwick is having work done at the moment. I also have to do some calculations to work out the weight of the plane, plus crates of cargo and the number of passengers. Then I put that with the route into a computer, plus the alternatives in case we get diverted, and the computer comes up with how much fuel we'll need. But, often at the last minute, we get notification of some more passengers so that requires a further calculation and more fuel.

I'm often asked if I have a degree in maths as I need to do so many calculations, but I haven't. Like me, most of my colleagues have studied science at university. You do need to have a good head for figures, though. I often think it would have been good to study people management, too.

The interior of the cockpit, where I and my co-pilot sit, is quite small and cramped. There's a practical reason for that – we need to be able to reach the controls, just in case one of us falls ill. But there's space to put our jackets in the cupboard at the back. Everything we need is more or less reachable without having to stand up.

I can't really move around during the flight. We used to have to get up to open the door if one of the cabin crew wanted to come in but now we can do that electronically. And we can see on a monitor who's at the door to the cockpit or the cabin behind.

Before I take off, I just need to check if there are any small defects on the plane. I receive a report of anything I need to be aware of, in which case I call for assistance. It can be just a little thing like a broken ice chiller in the front cabin and, if there are no real problems then we're ready for the people to come on board.

I've visited some wonderful places. What I like best, though, is flying at night. If the skies are clear, you can have stars above you and the lights of cities below you. And then there's the moonlight on the mountains. It's magical.

So, if you have any questions … [fade]

[pause]

Now you will hear Part Two again.

tone

[The recording is repeated.]

[pause]

That is the end of Part Two.

Now turn to Part Three.

[pause]

PART 3

You will hear five short extracts in which students are talking about a trip they have taken. For questions 19 to 23, choose from the list (A to H) what each student says about their trip. Use the letters only once. There are three extra letters which you do not need to use.

You now have thirty seconds to look at Part Three.

[pause]

tone

Speaker 1

My tour of the Highlands was just fantastic, and a great way to start off my year studying in Scotland. I swam in a freezing lake – stopped at the ruins of a medieval castle and chatted with the tour guide all the way home on the bus. He was a great character, really friendly, and took his responsibilities seriously. I learnt a lot, and without him, I wouldn't have had half as much fun. There's little doubt in my mind that I'll be returning there someday – they were some of the most beautiful places I've seen in my life.

[pause]

Speaker 2

It was the first time I'd set foot in mainland Europe, and in reality it was my first experience of real travel. I wasn't exactly prepared for the big city – for example I walked half a day to one of the main sights because I hadn't thought of using public transport. That's why it's one place I genuinely want to go back to but next time with friends and I'd take in some sights I may have missed. The trip does have one up on many of the other cities and countries that I've visited since, as it was the first time I'd realised how amazing travelling can be.

[pause]

Speaker 3

To be honest, I was a bit disappointed when I arrived in the city, partly because at the time it reminded me of every other major European city I'd seen, and partly because I was sharing a room in a youth hostel with five girls I didn't know who talked and laughed until the early hours. Looking back on it now, I realise I judged the city a bit too harshly. I actually had a great time riding the double-decker tour bus around during the day, and eating at little local restaurants in the evening. I also met some interesting people, and I might go back and stay with one of them.

[pause]

Speaker 4

My trip to London was spent with two buddies from high school; one who was studying in Holland, and one who was actually studying in London. It may not seem all that significant, but if you'd asked any of the three of us when we were back in high school what we'd be doing in the future, I seriously doubt any of us would've said meeting up in London while studying abroad. I think you see another side of your friends if you travel together, and we all feel even closer to each other than before. I'm sure we'll all go back one day.

[pause]

Speaker 5

I went to the capital twice, and the second time was with my family when they came over to visit towards the end of my second term. It was great, because my family paid for me to do everything that I was too poor to do the first time around. But more importantly, I was happy to be able to enjoy my travels with the people that mean the most to me. My parents had never been to the capital before, so were happy to visit all the main sights during the day and wander around soaking up the atmosphere in the evenings.

[pause]

Now you will hear Part Three again.

tone

[The recording is repeated.]

[pause]

That is the end of Part Three.

Now turn to Part Four.

[pause]

PART 4   *You will hear an interview with a musician called Jarrold Harding who's talking about his career. For questions 24 to 30, choose the best answer (A, B or C).*

You now have one minute to look at Part Four.

[pause]

tone

Interviewer: We are very pleased to welcome the violinist and conductor Jarrold Harding, who has come to tell us about how he began his career as a musician.
Jarrold: Hello.
Interviewer: Well first of all, Jarrold, how did your interest in music begin?
Jarrold: My father was a violinist in an orchestra, and from an early age I would go with him when they were rehearsing for concerts. I would sit with the violinists, and listen. I learned a lot, and everyone was very kind to me. I actually composed my first piece of music for the violin when I was six years old. My father treasured it!
Interviewer: And when did you start playing in public?
Jarrold: When I was around eight years old, my father started playing in a small orchestra at a holiday resort in the summer. All the family went with him – it was on the coast, and that way we had a break we couldn't have afforded otherwise. I sometimes went along to performances, and I played in my first concert there at the age of eleven, just for fun. My mother also played the piano in a hotel in the evenings.
Interviewer: So your mother was a musician, too? Tell us about her.
Jarrold: Sure. She was an amazing pianist! She knew all the music she played by heart – everything! And that was after playing it through just a couple of times to get it right. I learned that from her, and that's what I do on the violin, too – because I don't have to read the notes, I can concentrate on my playing and avoid errors.
Interviewer: And what made you interested in conducting?
Jarrold: From the very start, conductors fascinated me a great deal! I dreamt of becoming one from the first time I saw an orchestra. When I listened to recordings at home, I would conduct them! But my father insisted that I become a violinist, and he also taught me. So that's what I did, but I never gave up my old dream.
Interviewer: You studied music at one of the best colleges. Did you enjoy it?
Jarrold: I could do the violin playing anyway, of course, which my father had taught me. But then, so could everyone else. And, naturally, I perfected my technique at college and broadened the range of music I played. But some of the others found the discipline and commitment required of us too demanding. But because of my upbringing, I was used to that.
Interviewer: So what happened when you left college?

Jarrold: Well, just when I was about to start a career as a violinist, I started learning to be a conductor too! Even after college, I needed to carry on improving, so I was having private lessons with a professional violinist. And his wife – although not a professional musician – taught me conducting technique. She insisted that I took lessons from a teacher she knew who had many well-known conductors as students. He himself wasn't a well-known conductor, but as an instructor he was the best, and very enthusiastic.

Interviewer: Since then, you've become well known as both a violinist and a conductor. Has it been difficult to have both these careers?

Jarrold: On the contrary – I've learned so much from the conductors I've played with as a violin soloist. Even when one plays the same violin piece often, it's still always different every time. One can therefore learn a great deal, especially as I've had the good fortune to practically always play under the best conductors in the world. And I haven't only learned from seeing and hearing them, but I've always taken the time to consult them, to discuss the smallest details with them, and to continuously improve myself.

Interviewer: Well, unfortunately we've run out of time – but thank you very much, it's been a great pleasure speaking to you. And the very best of luck in the future!

Jarrold: Thank you!

[pause]

Now you will hear Part Four again.

tone

[The recording is repeated.]

[pause]

That is the end of Part Four.

There will now be a pause of five minutes for you to copy your answers onto the separate answer sheet. Be sure to follow the numbering of all the questions. I shall remind you when there is one minute left, so that you are sure to finish in time.

[Teacher, pause the recording here for five minutes. Remind students when they have one minute left.]

That is the end of the test. Please stop now. Your supervisor will now collect all the question papers and answer sheets.

Test 3 Key

Reading and Use of English (1 hour 15 minutes)

Part 1

1 B   2 D   3 B   4 A   5 C   6 D   7 B   8 C

Part 2

9 one   10 as   11 what   12 of   13 In   14 been   15 order   16 amount

Part 3

17 impossible   18 exhausting   19 breathless   20 marvellous   21 enjoyable
22 unlike   23 pleasure   24 equally

Part 4

25 play BETTER tennis | than he OR play tennis BETTER | than he
26 is/are | (being) BOUGHT from OR can | be BOUGHT from
27 was PRAISED | by the coach
28 to get | in TOUCH with
29 go on SALE until/before/till OR be on/for SALE | until/before/till
30 if | it had not/hadn't BEEN

Part 5

31 D   32 C   33 B   34 A   35 D   36 C

Part 6

37 F   38 C   39 G   40 A   41 E   42 D

Part 7

43 B   44 A   45 D   46 D   47 B   48 A   49 C   50 B   51 D   52 C

Writing (1 hour 20 minutes)

Candidate responses are marked using the assessment scale on pages 107–108.

Listening (approximately 40 minutes)

Part 1

1 A   2 A   3 B   4 A   5 A   6 A   7 B   8 B

Part 2

9 May   **10** safety   **11** helmet   **12** seats   **13** 700 / seven hundred   **14** gloves
15 calm   **16** silver   **17** feather   **18** T-shirt

Part 3

19 H   20 E   21 F   22 C   23 G

Part 4

24 B   25 A   26 C   27 B   28 A   29 B   30 A

Transcript   *This is the Cambridge English: First, Test Three.*

I am going to give you the instructions for this test. I shall introduce each part of the test and give you time to look at the questions. At the start of each piece you will hear this sound:

tone

You will hear each piece twice.

Remember, while you are listening, write your answers on the question paper. You will have five minutes at the end of the test to copy your answers onto the separate answer sheet.

There will now be a pause. Please ask any questions now, because you must not speak during the test.

[pause]

Now open your question paper and look at Part One.

[pause]

PART 1   *You will hear people talking in eight different situations. For questions 1 to 8, choose the best answer (A, B or C).*

Question 1   *One.*
You hear a young actor talking about a colleague.

[pause]

tone

Just watching her work is very useful. I've only been acting for about a year so I've got so much to learn. When you meet someone who's as famous as she is, there's always a bit of nerves. She's an intelligent actor and everything she does seems so effortless. As I've got such a small part in the drama, I get to stand around a lot during the scenes and it means I can watch and learn from her. She's very composed when she's acting; she takes her time to say her lines.

[pause]

tone

[The recording is repeated.]

[pause]

Question 2

Two.
You hear two friends talking about a colleague.

[pause]

tone

Woman: I don't know how he does it – he gets into the office before everyone else in the morning, and he's also always the last to leave. He must be exhausted all the time!

Man: He seems pretty fit, though – and whenever I see him at the weekends, he looks relaxed and happy. Maybe he just likes getting everything done before he goes home.

Woman: Yeah, maybe you're right … but he earns just the same as we do, and that's not much.

Man: It's not too bad, though, is it? And I think he'll be promoted before any of the rest of us are – he's obviously very keen!

Woman: There's no denying that!

[pause]

tone

[The recording is repeated.]

[pause]

Question 3

Three.
You hear an author talking about his new book.

[pause]

tone

Thanks for inviting me to come on the programme and talk about my new book. I thought the book might never happen when I was sitting at my desk day after day. I wished the words would simply flow out like they did when I was writing my other books. Sometimes I wondered if I'd ever get it finished. Of course, I know it's unlikely to be become a best-seller, but I hope that my loyal readers will enjoy it. They'll recognise some of the characters from my first novel, older and wiser – at least in some cases!

[pause]

tone

[The recording is repeated.]

[pause]

Question 4   *Four.*
You hear two friends talking about something they saw on TV.

[pause]

tone

Man: It's funny really, but I just didn't get it. Everyone was talking about it, but I just thought it was silly.
Woman: You mean you wanted more information?
Man: Exactly! I mean what's the point of something like that? It didn't even make me laugh.
Woman: Oh come on, you have to admit it was pretty funny!
Man: Well I didn't think so. And it was annoying the way everybody whistled the tune all the time. Why on earth would that make me buy something?
Woman: I think you're too serious sometimes. It was just a bit of fun. If you want to find out more, then look on the internet.

[pause]

tone

[The recording is repeated.]

[pause]

Question 5   *Five.*
You hear an office manager talking about her work.

[pause]

tone

You know how it is … as soon as you've finished one project, you have to get started on something else, and it's often something completely different. I don't find that a problem though, and I enjoy the fact that I can get it done effectively – after all, I've been in this job for a long time so I think I can say I know what I'm doing! I wish that was true of the people I'm working with – I reckon if I didn't keep checking, they'd never get on with things! Though I guess I'm not feeling very motivated about this project either.

[pause]

tone

[The recording is repeated.]

[pause]

Question 6

Six.
You overhear two friends talking in a restaurant.

[pause]

tone

Man: Hmm! Delicious soup!
Woman: You think so? It's a bit hot, isn't it?
Man: What do you mean, hot? Too many spices, or the temperature?
Woman: It burned my mouth.
Man: Well, you should have had something else. There was plenty to choose from.
Woman: There may have been for you, but don't forget I'm a vegetarian – there wasn't much there for me.
Man: But at least we haven't paid a fortune for it.
Woman: Um, I couldn't even make it at home for that price. But I still think we should go somewhere else next time …

[pause]

tone

[The recording is repeated.]

[pause]

Question 7

Seven.
You hear a woman talking about her neighbours' holiday photographs.

[pause]

tone

They always invite us round for dinner after they've been on holiday, and show us all the photos they've taken. I didn't like the dinner much, but of course I didn't say anything. They go to some interesting places, and they actually do pretty well considering they don't have expensive equipment, or any training as photographers. I wish I could remember the name of the place they went to this summer – that's really annoying – I should have written it down. I'll have to ask them next time I see them.

[pause]

tone

[The recording is repeated.]

[pause]

Question 8

Eight.
You hear two friends talking about a concert they've just been to.

[pause]

tone

Woman:	I really enjoyed that, didn't you, despite the technical problems at the beginning.
Man:	Wonderful. Spanish flamenco music just makes you want to get up and dance.
Woman:	I noticed you standing up at one stage.
Man:	Yeah, but that was to get a better view.
Woman:	Ahh – yes, pity we were at the back. But it was all that was available when I bought the tickets on Friday.
Man:	I know, but next time we must book earlier.
Woman:	It was very hot in there.
Man:	Did that bother you? I just kept thinking it was like summer in Spain. I loved all the singing and the rhythm of the sticks they beat on the floor.
Woman:	Me too.

[pause]

tone

[The recording is repeated.]

[pause]

That is the end of Part One.

Now turn to Part Two.

[pause]

PART 2   *You will hear a man called Henry Lee giving a talk about the first time he went skydiving. For questions 9 to 18, complete the sentences with a word or short phrase.*

You now have forty-five seconds to look at Part Two.

[pause]

tone

Hello, my name is Henry Lee and I've been skydiving for several years now but I'm here today to tell you about my first experience. The idea of skydiving is that you jump out of a plane wearing a parachute but the parachute doesn't open immediately. I'd always wanted to learn to skydive and when I was twenty, a friend bought me a skydiving lesson for my birthday. Now, my birthday is in December when the weather isn't right for this type of sport so I decided to wait a bit until the weather improved around March. Anyway, as it turned out, it wasn't until May that I finally got round to it.

I arrived at the skydiving club for my lesson and found that there were around seven other people who were jumping that day. We all had to sign a number of forms, and we looked at a short video about basic technique before having a presentation about safety. Then I was introduced to David, my instructor. As I was a beginner, I wouldn't be jumping out of the plane alone. I would be attached to David and he would be in total control of the jump. David gave me most of the stuff I would need to wear – some overalls to wear over my clothes and a pair of goggles and, crucially, a helmet. I didn't need to have a parachute as David would wear one.

There were thirteen of us on the plane; four of us were beginners with our instructors, and three solo jumpers and two cameramen who would film the dive for the club. It was an old cargo plane, without windows and, interestingly, there were no seats – just some metal boxes which were normally used for luggage – so it was quite uncomfortable. The plane trip was fine and during it I asked David how long he'd been skydiving. He said he'd started about three years ago and had seven hundred jumps to his name. Other guys on the plane though, had done over a thousand.

When we were a few minutes away from jumping I attached myself to David, who was wearing a system of belts called a harness. I also put on a pair of gloves which I'd been told to bring with me. I'd been very excited when we took off and I thought I would feel absolutely terrified when the plane door was opened. But actually I was completely calm. Once we reached the right height above the ground, the pilot cried out, 'Door!' and the more advanced divers just jumped out of the plane. When I reached the door I sat down in it and looked out over the ground below. I could see a farmer's fields and a large house. What caught my eye was a river which looked silver rather than bright blue or dark grey, winding its way across the countryside. David and I were the last people out of the plane. We jumped with me facing downwards attached to David's body. There were about forty or fifty seconds until he opened the parachute.

The landing was a bit different from what I thought it would be. I thought you'd hit the ground hard and fast and have to try hard not to break a leg. My landing was actually more like a feather falling to earth and I didn't realise I was on the ground until I saw the parachute all around me. Everyone who completes the jump successfully is given a bag which contains a certificate, a discount voucher and a photograph of their jump. Only when I got home did I realise there was a T-shirt at the bottom of the bag. That was a nice surprise. I put my name down on the club notice board to have more lessons. My first skydiving experience was one that I'll never forget and I'd recommend the sport to anyone.

[pause]

Now you will hear Part Two again.

tone

[The recording is repeated.]

[pause]

That is the end of Part Two.

Now turn to Part Three.

[pause]

PART 3   *You will hear five short extracts in which students are talking about the experience of living and studying away from home. For questions 19 to 23, choose from the list (A to H) what each student says. Use the letters only once. There are three extra letters which you do not need to use.*

You now have thirty seconds to look at Part Three.

[pause]

tone

Speaker 1

Coming from a mountain village about sixty kilometres away, and not knowing anyone in the city, I had no choice really – I had to ask for a place in a college residence. I knew it wouldn't be easy making new friends, but I was assured I'd be with my classmates. It was a surprise to find the other guys in my block were all studying different things. Actually though, we were all the same age and into sports and stuff, so we got on really well from day one. It was a pity we all went our separate ways after that first year together. I should've made more effort to stay in touch.

[pause]

Speaker 2

I wanted to study fashion, so I had to come to the capital, but it was hard leaving my friends back home. My older sister studied here too. She made friends really quickly because she's really into sports and joined loads of clubs. But I've always been quite shy, so I didn't do that. Fortunately, the college accommodation office found me a room in a residence and I got friendly with the other girls living there. I don't know how I'd have got on at a big university, but here everyone knows each other – so you get to know people you wouldn't normally have that much in common with – it's nice.

[pause]

Speaker 3

In my first few weeks here, I came down with a heavy cold that meant I couldn't go out much. I'd been put in a student residence with a bunch of younger guys who were all studying theatre – so as a scientist I had nothing in common with them – they weren't even into football! So I really needed to get to know my classmates better – yet there I was stuck in my room coughing and sneezing. I spent a lot of time chatting to friends back home on the internet. Anyway, in a big college like this, you eventually have to make friends – so it all sorted itself out in the end.

[pause]

Speaker 4

I was put in a student residence at first with people I didn't get along with that well. I mean, we didn't fall out or anything, but I didn't hang out with them either. I don't know what I'd have done if I hadn't signed up for volleyball training with the college team. It's a whole lot easier making friends with people who share your interests than with people who share your kitchen! The only downside for me in that first term was that I spent too much time on court and not enough in the library! I don't regret it, but had to make up for lost time later on!

[pause]

Speaker 5

The people I hung out with in the first few weeks didn't become close friends actually. We were just people who happened to be thrown together in the same residence, but it was good to have someone to chat to when I got in from lectures. We still play tennis occasionally and I get invited to their parties, but I soon moved out to go live with some guys on my course. That was a big mistake actually. With friends at school, it was great to study together in the evenings – but I soon found that the last thing I wanted to talk about when I got back from lectures was economics!

[pause]

Now you will hear Part Three again.

tone

[The recording is repeated.]

[pause]

That is the end of Part Three.

Now turn to Part Four.

[pause]

PART 4   *You will hear an interview with a student athlete called Chelsea Matthews, who plays soccer for her college. For questions 24 to 30, choose the best answer (A, B or C).*

You now have one minute to look at Part Four.

[pause]

tone

Interviewer: I'm talking to student athlete, Chelsea Matthews. Chelsea, what impact does playing soccer have on your life?

Chelsea: For the past two years, I've played soccer for my college. And we train extremely hard almost every day during the year. We can only keep up by doing extra work at home. We travel by bus for hours and hours, missing out on typical college events and we sometimes spend our precious vacation time training abroad. But I love it.

Interviewer: How young were you when you started playing soccer?

Chelsea: Six, and I always dreamt of playing in college. By the time I was sixteen, I'd picked out my college, and started my training. While other teenagers were focused on parties, I was already planning my life as a college student-athlete. It has to be done that early, or you'll miss so much, and won't get through all the formalities that make you eligible to play. The one thing sports associations love more than trophies is paperwork.

Interviewer: When does your year start at college?

Chelsea: Well, because of where soccer falls in the school year (August to October), I have to arrive at my college about a month before classes start.

Interviewer: Are you happy about that?

Chelsea: Yes I'm used to it. On August first me and my team-mates return, and get straight back into school mode. By August second, I'll be up at six am to start my training. Every college sport has a two-week 'pre-season' which is tough but essential. We run, lift, pass, kick, run more, and, basically, kill ourselves. Our coach is good, though, and keeps us motivated in spite of the pain.

Interviewer: Do you have time to have some fun after training?

Chelsea: I don't know about other sports teams but we do have a little fun as a team after workouts. There's no partying in pre-season though. By the time seven pm rolls around, we're all so weary we just get in bed, crash, and know no more until the alarm goes off. Movies are out, and if it weren't for the Internet, we'd never even get to watch TV! And it only gets harder once school starts.

Interviewer: Are you allowed to miss class?

Chelsea: During the season, thanks to away games, we frequently miss class. Other students see us athletes going up to professors, saying we'll be away, and they're probably jealous of the number of excused absences we get. But honestly, missing class is the worst part of being an athlete. First, our grades have to remain high or we could lose our place on the team. Second, the head of faculty allows a maximum number of hours we can take off class, and it's not that many.

Interviewer: How have you personally managed?

Chelsea: I basically taught myself Business Calculus in my freshman year, because I missed some classes due to away games and had to be able to understand what was going on when I got back. You can trust me on this: trying to read, write, calculate, or draw on a moving bus with thirty other girls at ten thirty at night isn't the best way to get a grade A. And because of all those absences, when I get sick (which happens when you're on the road so much) I still have to go to class.

Interviewer: In conclusion, any regrets?

Chelsea: It's hard work to try and balance school, soccer and a social life. But I love playing soccer, and I love my team. It's thirty girls who all want the same thing: to win. We work together both off and on the field; we run together, we cheer each other on, we help each other with studies. My team are my best friends. I chose this life, and it's given me ambition, shown me I must try to be the best – academically, athletically and personally.

[pause]

Now you will hear Part Four again.

tone

[The recording is repeated.]

[pause]

That is the end of Part Four.

There will now be a pause of five minutes for you to copy your answers onto the separate answer sheet. Be sure to follow the numbering of all the questions. I shall remind you when there is one minute left, so that you are sure to finish in time.

[Teacher, pause the recording here for five minutes. Remind students when they have one minute left.]

That is the end of the test. Please stop now. Your supervisor will now collect all the question papers and answer sheets.

Test 4 Key

Reading and Use of English (1 hour 15 minutes)

Part 1

1 B   2 D   3 A   4 D   5 D   6 C   7 B   8 B

Part 2

9 As/While   10 like   11 what   12 which/that   13 and   14 a
15 since   16 one

Part 3

17 objective   18 description   19 decisions   20 personality   21 unconsciously
22 ease   23 variety   24 enthusiastic

Part 4

25 how MUCH | the trips
26 able to | COME up with
27 to GIVE | (careful) thought/consideration to
28 on (walking) | EVEN when/though/after it
29 HARDLY any tickets | left/remaining/(still) available
30 a/any CHANCE | of getting

Part 5

31 A   32 D   33 B   34 B   35 A   36 C

Part 6

37 E   38 D   39 G   40 A   41 F   42 B

Part 7

43 A   44 D   45 C   46 A   47 B   48 D   49 C   50 A
51 C   52 D

Writing (1 hour 20 minutes)

Candidate responses are marked using the assessment scale on pages 107–108.

Listening (approximately 40 minutes)

Part 1

1 A   2 A   3 C   4 C   5 B   6 B   7 B   8 A

Part 2

9 horse(-)riding   10 starter   11 (green) badge(s)   12 35/thirty-five (pounds)
13 gym   14 (sports)(-)bag   15 first(-)team   16 notice(-)board   17 party
18 discount

Part 3

19 D   20 G   21 B   22 E   23 F

Part 4

24 B   25 A   26 A   27 C   28 B   29 C   30 B

Transcript *This is the Cambridge English: First, Test Four.*

I am going to give you the instructions for this test. I shall introduce each part of the test and give you time to look at the questions. At the start of each piece you will hear this sound:

  tone

You will hear each piece twice.

Remember, while you are listening, write your answers on the question paper. You will have five minutes at the end of the test to copy your answers onto the separate answer sheet.

There will now be a pause. Please ask any questions now, because you must not speak during the test.

[pause]

Now open your question paper and look at Part One.

[pause]

PART 1   *You will hear people talking in eight different situations. For questions 1 to 8, choose the best answer (A, B or C).*

Question 1   *One.*
You hear a sportsperson talking about her sporting career.

[pause]

tone

When I work so hard for any competition and then it's over, the following weeks can be really difficult – quite an anti-climax. But then the next competition comes along and I get straight back into training. But this time it'll be different. I'll miss it, of course I will. But at some point in your career you have to say enough is enough and I wanted to finish at the top of my game. I don't have any plans yet but it won't be anything connected with sport. I've always wanted to be a writer so perhaps I'll do a writing course next.

[pause]

tone

[The recording is repeated.]

[pause]

Question 2   *Two.*
You hear two friends talking about a laboratory experiment.

[pause]

tone

Woman: How do you think the experiment went, then?
Man: Not sure, really. It was pretty exciting at the time, but now we have to work out what it all means.
Woman: Yes, it always does take a while to analyse the results. I just hope we did it all properly.
Man: Yeah, that's what concerns me – if we got anything wrong, then we'll have to start all over again, which would be a pain.
Woman: True, but I think we were very careful. I can't see why we should have to repeat it all.
Man: I hope you're right!

[pause]

tone

[The recording is repeated.]

[pause]

Question 3   *Three.*
                    You overhear a student calling his university department.

                    [pause]

                    tone

                    Hello, I wonder if I could talk to someone about the History of Art course? My teacher told me I could call your department if I needed to discuss anything – and I do. The trouble is, I'm finding it difficult to get all the work for this course module done on time. Even though the classes are great – and that's very much because of the teacher, Mr Flynn – I just can't keep up. So I wondered if I could come in and see the head of department about the problem.

                    [pause]

                    tone

                    [The recording is repeated.]

                    [pause]

Question 4   *Four.*
                    You hear two friends talking about a website.

                    [pause]

                    tone

Woman: Did you have a look at that study skills website I told you about?
Man: Yes, I did.
Woman: And what did you think?
Man: Well, I had no trouble finding my way around it, which was good.
Woman: Is that all? Did you find any ideas you could use yourself?
Man: Not really, I'm afraid.
Woman: Oh dear, it sounds as if you found it a bit dull.
Man: Well ... it's just that I've seen a lot of those ideas before. It's hard for people to come up with anything new, I suppose.
Woman: That's true ... if you come across a good one, you'll let me know, won't you?
Man: Sure!

                    [pause]

                    tone

                    [The recording is repeated.]

                    [pause]

Question 5   *Five.*
You hear a man talking about his decision to become a singer.

[pause]

tone

I don't come from a particularly musical family and it was very difficult to tell my parents I wanted to become a singer because they obviously didn't want me to do it. I'm sure my mother would have been equally annoyed if I'd gone into classical music. She just thought music wasn't a viable career choice. She's always had faith in me as a person and knows I'm very determined and would succeed whatever I chose to do but she wanted me to get some qualifications behind me first. Once I started to become successful she was grudgingly happy for me, but she was still convinced it wouldn't last.

[pause]

tone

[The recording is repeated.]

[pause]

Question 6   *Six.*
You overhear a man calling a TV shop.

[pause]

tone

Hello, I came into your shop a few days ago to look at TVs. You didn't have the one I wanted in stock, but you said you could order it for me. My name's Hogg, Jim Hogg. I paid when I was in the shop, and I got a message just now saying the TV's arrived. When I came in the other day, your colleague said one of your van drivers could drop it off one evening next week. I'm usually back from work after six, so ... [fade]

[pause]

tone

[The recording is repeated.]

[pause]

Question 7   *Seven.*
You hear two friends talking about a meal.

[pause]

tone

Man:	Well, that meal was OK – I can't manage a dessert. How was your fried fish, Anna?
Anna:	It was quite nice though it could have been hotter. I'm not sure that salad went with it, either. I'd have preferred some cooked vegetables. Yours looked really good, with your steak.
Man:	Yeah – they would've been a much better combination with your meal. Maybe we should've swapped – I like salad with steak. Anyway, it was a pretty reasonable price.
Anna:	Yours was – mine was a bit much, I reckon.
Man:	We both had a lot of food on our plates, though – can't complain about that.
Anna:	I guess not.

[pause]

tone

[The recording is repeated.]

[pause]

Question 8

Eight.
You hear a college lecturer talking to a student.

[pause]

tone

So that's good news, isn't it? You won't actually need to hand the project in until next month now, which gives you a couple of extra weeks. I know you can do it all yourself, and I'm sure it'll be very good. You've always produced excellent work in the past, haven't you? Everything you need to know has been covered in the lessons, and there are plenty of books in the library. You can also use the computers there if you need to go online for more information. So there's really nothing to worry about, is there?

[pause]

tone

[The recording is repeated.]

[pause]

That is the end of Part One.

Now turn to Part Two.

[pause]

PART 2   *You will hear a girl called Kyra talking about the badminton club she belongs to. For questions 9 to 18, complete the sentences with a word or short phrase.*

You now have forty-five seconds to look at Part Two.

[pause]

tone

Hi there. I'm Kyra and I'm a member of the local Badminton club. I'm here to tell you all about the club, and hopefully find a few new members.

So, first of all, why badminton? Well, I'd say whatever your level of fitness, you should definitely consider taking up badminton. It's a sociable sport that you can play at any age, whilst requiring very little specific training or equipment.

Before I took up badminton, I'd never been very sporty, despite the fact that my brother's a skateboarding champion and my parents are very keen on tennis. The only sport I'd ever really enjoyed was horse-riding. But I didn't even keep that up once I'd left school. It was a friend who talked me into trying badminton, and I've never looked back.

Regular badminton sessions are held every Wednesday evening at the Sportsworld Centre. But next Sunday we're holding what's known as a 'starter' session. Now this isn't a normal session and nor is it a training session – instead it's a chance for prospective members to come along, have a game and see if they like the sport. Obviously we hope they will, and that they'll sign up – but there's no obligation.

So why not come along and find out what it's all about? There's nothing to pay. You should just wear comfortable clothes and trainers. Don't worry if you don't have proper sports gear – and of course you'll be given a racquet and shuttlecocks, and be introduced to a partner, if you're on your own. If you do have any questions, however, just ask a committee member. Everyone at Sportsworld has to wear a badge; you'll be given one at the door, but committee members wear special green ones, so you can't miss them.

If you do decide to join the badminton club, then you'll pay an annual fee of thirty-five pounds. Membership of Sportsworld, with access to certain facilities at the centre usually costs forty-five pounds, but it's included in the badminton club membership for new members – so that's really good value for money. This gives you, amongst other things, free use of the gym, but not the swimming pool. All our regular sessions are held at Sportsworld, although matches are sometimes held elsewhere.

Oh and I nearly forgot, we also have a shop where you can buy a second-hand racquet or a T-shirt and other stuff, and when you join our club we'll give you a free sports bag – so it's a good deal all round.

Our regular sessions are open to all members – those who enjoy the social side of the sport, as well as those who are looking for competitive games in order to improve. For our first team, we also offer coaching once a week on Monday evenings from eight to ten. That's a dedicated session just for them.

At other times, you might want to come along for a game, and there are sometimes courts available at Sportsworld. Although we have a website, which is regularly updated with club news, it doesn't yet have a court booking facility, unfortunately – so you need to check the club's notice-board at Sportsworld to see what's available.

The club also holds regular social events – and for many people that's an important aspect of membership. We put on quiz nights, for example, and often meet up for a meal in a local restaurant. The highlight of the year, however, is the party. We raise a lot of money for the club selling tickets for that.

So I hope I've managed to convince you that the badminton club is worth giving a try, and that you'll come along and find out more about us. As a final incentive, if you go up to the Sportsworld café on Sunday and say you're taking part in the badminton club session, you won't get a free drink, but you will get a discount. You see – we really want you to come!

So now, before I pass you over to ….. [fade]

[pause]

Now you will hear Part Two again.

tone

[The recording is repeated.]

[pause]

That is the end of Part Two.

Now turn to Part Three.

[pause]

PART 3

You will hear five short extracts in which people are talking about why their businesses became successful. For questions 19 to 23, choose from the list (A to H) what each speaker says. Use the letters only once. There are three extra letters which you do not need to use.

You now have thirty seconds to look at Part Three.

[pause]

tone

Speaker 1

I started making dolls filled with scented herbs for my daughter's friends in 2008. They proved a great hit because parents discovered that the dolls helped their children to sleep at night, so I started my own business making them. I soon couldn't keep up with demand from satisfied customers. I was lucky because I had a great product and I could prove that there was a market for it, so it wasn't difficult to find an investor. If I hadn't been able to do that, I'd still be doing this as a hobby and I certainly wouldn't be employing twenty people. The business has really boomed and last year we doubled our turnover.

[pause]

Speaker 2

When I bought my first taxi a couple of years ago, I saw it as a way to get out of my career in sales. I'd been thinking about doing it for years, but I felt anxious about the financial commitment. I didn't have a lot of money back then, so I talked to all my contacts – entrepreneurs who ran their own companies – and asked for their suggestions about running a business. They were really generous with their time. Now that I run a very successful taxi business, I've even been asked to give talks to students on business courses. You know, give them a bit of advice and feedback on their work.

[pause]

Speaker 3

I've always loved designing gardens and I knew I didn't want to work for someone else, so I put a small advert in the local paper and within a week I'd got my first client. It's not easy persuading people to employ a garden designer because it's something a lot of people think they can do themselves. Three years ago, I started distributing leaflets at the weekends, when most people are doing their gardening. I was able to talk to them in person about their gardens. I got a lot more business that way and it was much better than an ad in the newspaper. My business has really taken off since then and I've got five people working for me now.

[pause]

Speaker 4

My company is the main marketplace for new and used musical instruments. We sell to everyone from complete beginners to some of the most famous musicians in the industry and I've doubled my turnover in five years without adding any new stores or employing any new staff. Few companies approach things the way I do. See, most music stores provide temporary employment for people who want to be professional musicians. I, on the other hand, invest in my workforce and want them to develop as musicians while they're here. That's why I built a recording studio, which they can use too. When people are passionate about what they do, they're happy – and if they're happy, they sell more!

[pause]

Speaker 5

I always had big dreams of working in the entertainment industry. I took a job with an event planner and in my free time I began making props and costumes. The turning point was when I began to see that I had a range of skills other people didn't have. I also knew that advertising myself as a specialist in designing props and entertainment costumes would set me apart from others. Within three years I was earning more money from sewing than from my full-time job so I resigned and concentrated on my business. I took on more contracts and earned eighty thousand dollars in my first year.

[pause]

Now you will hear Part Three again.

tone

[The recording is repeated.]

[pause]

That is the end of Part Three.

Now turn to Part Four.

[pause]

PART 4

You will hear a radio interview with a man called Tony Little, who makes wildlife films and works for a wildlife conservation organisation called The Nature Trust. For questions 24 to 30, choose the best answer (A, B or C).

You now have one minute to look at Part Four.

[pause]

tone

Interviewer: With me today I have Tony Little, who is well known for making wildlife documentaries and has just been made President of The Nature Trust. Tony, I've got a lot of questions here sent in by our listeners. The first one is: What do you think is going to be your hardest challenge during your time as president?

Tony: Well, I think most people nowadays understand what The Nature Trust is about. We have quite a few neighbourhood groups in the UK now, but these consist mainly of adults and what I want to do is get kids to take an interest too – not always as easy as you might imagine. You know, helping out just for the fun of it – clearing woods and counting different bird species, things like that.

Interviewer: Another listener wants to know: Is there any special area that you would say needs attention most – for example our use of plastic?

Tony: People are doing quite a bit to help conservation and the environment. However, what we do forget is the rubbish we pump into the sea. The amount of plastic waste we find on beaches is horrendous. And this causes serious problems to wildlife. Changing to paper bags would help enormously, but this might take some time as people are so used to having plastic ones.

Interviewer: Someone has asked about your new website, Nature Talk. Can you tell us about that?

Tony: It's a project we're launching next month. We're confining ourselves first of all to animals which have a healthy population. There'll be maps on the website so you'll be able to pinpoint where these animals live and information about those areas – whether it's a forest or whatever. We're not expecting you to actually go and visit them.

Interviewer: You're known for your work with wildlife. Susan Smith wants to know: What have you achieved that you are most proud of?

Tony: Actually, one of my most popular films was the one I did on lions but I didn't feel it got anywhere near, in terms of being closest to my heart, to the time I spent rescuing orphan monkeys. The special sanctuary I set up won a world nature prize. A close second would be the research project I was involved with on whales in the South Atlantic. I spent quite a bit of time there and it was brilliant.

Interviewer: I have a letter from Peter McDonald, who wants to become a cameraman. Any advice to give him?

Tony: Well, Peter, first of all, let me say, the financial rewards can be great if you get the right pictures. When you start out though, it'll take you some time to get your name known, so jobs will be few and far between. You'll need to stick with it. It's interesting how many people think the job involves sitting in a tree for weeks waiting for an animal to appear, but that isn't always the case and shouldn't put you off applying to be a cameraman.

Interviewer: Many listeners have asked: Is there any particular equipment that they should get if they want to be a naturalist?

Tony: I guess most people would think it's a camera. I obviously have a large number of different models and they're quite expensive. But I think any type will do, even a cheap one these days is fine. What I wouldn't be without though are my binoculars, so get a top quality pair. Another useful item is a good pair of walking boots, but they aren't top of the list.

Interviewer: So, a question from me now: What about the future?

Tony: Well, I have lots of ideas for new TV programmes, but not ones about mammals. I think my role should be to persuade people that wildlife isn't just about big, exotic animals. I know that tigers and polar bears are endangered but, you know, so are a number of small insects and also plants which can be found in local parks and gardens. We must make sure people don't forget them either.

Interviewer: That's great. Well, my thanks to … [fade]

[pause]

Now you will hear Part Four again.

tone

[The recording is repeated.]

[pause]

That is the end of Part Four.

There will now be a pause of five minutes for you to copy your answers onto the separate answer sheet. Be sure to follow the numbering of all the questions. I shall remind you when there is one minute left, so that you are sure to finish in time.

[Teacher, pause the recording here for five minutes. Remind students when they have one minute left.]

That is the end of the test. Please stop now. Your supervisor will now collect all the question papers and answer sheets.

CAMBRIDGE ENGLISH
Language Assessment
Part of the University of Cambridge

Do not write in this box

SAMPLE

Candidate Name
If not already printed, write name in CAPITALS and complete the Candidate No. grid (in pencil).

Candidate Signature

Examination Title

Centre

Supervisor:
If the candidate is ABSENT or has WITHDRAWN shade here ▭

Centre No.

Candidate No.

Examination Details

Candidate Answer Sheet

Instructions

Use a PENCIL (B or HB).

Rub out any answer you wish to change using an eraser.

Parts 1, 5, 6 and **7:**
Mark ONE letter for each question.

For example, if you think **B** is the right answer to the question, mark your answer sheet like this:

Parts 2, 3 and **4:**
Write your answer clearly in CAPITAL LETTERS.

For Parts 2 and 3 write one letter in each box. For example:

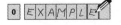

Part 1

1	A	B	C	D
2	A	B	C	D
3	A	B	C	D
4	A	B	C	D
5	A	B	C	D
6	A	B	C	D
7	A	B	C	D
8	A	B	C	D

Part 2

Do not write below here

9		9 1 0 u
10		10 1 0 u
11		11 1 0 u
12		12 1 0 u
13		13 1 0 u
14		14 1 0 u
15		15 1 0 u
16		16 1 0 u

Continues over ➡

FCE R

DP802

© UCLES 2014 Photocopiable

167

Part 3

		Do not write below here
17		17 1 0 u
18		18 1 0 u
19		19 1 0 u
20		20 1 0 u
21		21 1 0 u
22		22 1 0 u
23		23 1 0 u
24		24 1 0 u

Part 4

		Do not write below here
25		25 2 1 0 u
26		26 2 1 0 u
27		27 2 1 0 u
28		28 2 1 0 u
29		29 2 1 0 u
30		30 2 1 0 u

Part 5

31	A	B	C	D
32	A	B	C	D
33	A	B	C	D
34	A	B	C	D
35	A	B	C	D
36	A	B	C	D

Part 6

37	A	B	C	D	E	F	G
38	A	B	C	D	E	F	G
39	A	B	C	D	E	F	G
40	A	B	C	D	E	F	G
41	A	B	C	D	E	F	G
42	A	B	C	D	E	F	G

Part 7

43	A	B	C	D	E	F
44	A	B	C	D	E	F
45	A	B	C	D	E	F
46	A	B	C	D	E	F
47	A	B	C	D	E	F
48	A	B	C	D	E	F
49	A	B	C	D	E	F
50	A	B	C	D	E	F
51	A	B	C	D	E	F
52	A	B	C	D	E	F

© UCLES 2014 Photocopiable

 **CAMBRIDGE ENGLISH**
Language Assessment
Part of the University of Cambridge

Do not write in this box

SAMPLE

Candidate Name
If not already printed, write name
in CAPITALS and complete the
Candidate No. grid (in pencil).

Candidate Signature

Examination Title

Centre

Supervisor:

If the candidate is ABSENT or has WITHDRAWN shade here ⊂⊃

Centre No.

Candidate No.

Examination Details

Candidate Answer Sheet

Instructions

Use a PENCIL (B or HB).
Rub out any answer you wish to change using an eraser.

Parts 1, 3 and 4:
Mark ONE letter for each question.

For example, if you think **B** is the right answer to the question, mark your answer sheet like this:

Part 2:
Write your answer clearly in CAPITAL LETTERS.

Write one letter or number in each box.
If the answer has more than one word, leave one box empty between words.

For example:

Turn this sheet over to start.

© UCLES 2014 Photocopiable

Sample answer sheet: Listening

Part 1

1	A	B	C
2	A	B	C
3	A	B	C
4	A	B	C
5	A	B	C
6	A	B	C
7	A	B	C
8	A	B	C

Part 2 (Remember to write in CAPITAL LETTERS or numbers)

Do not write below here

9		9 1 0 u
10		10 1 0 u
11		11 1 0 u
12		12 1 0 u
13		13 1 0 u
14		14 1 0 u
15		15 1 0 u
16		16 1 0 u
17		17 1 0 u
18		18 1 0 u

Part 3

19	A	B	C	D	E	F	G	H
20	A	B	C	D	E	F	G	H
21	A	B	C	D	E	F	G	H
22	A	B	C	D	E	F	G	H
23	A	B	C	D	E	F	G	H

Part 4

24	A	B	C
25	A	B	C
26	A	B	C
27	A	B	C
28	A	B	C
29	A	B	C
30	A	B	C

© UCLES 2014 Photocopiable

Thanks and acknowledgements

The authors and publishers acknowledge the following sources of copyright material and are grateful for the permissions granted. While every effort has been made, it has not always been possible to identify the sources of all the material used, or to trace all copyright holders. If any omissions are brought to our notice, we will be happy to include the appropriate acknowledgements on reprinting.

Text Acknowledgements

Gizmag for the text on p. 10 adapted from 'Japan's two-stand folding bicycle' by Rick Martin, *Gizmag* 10/02/2010. Reproduced with permission; The Guardian for the text on p. 14 adapted from 'I had to make time for him: Alfred Brendel on Kit Armstrong' by Alan Rusbridger, *The Guardian* 02/06/2011, © Guardian News & Media Ltd 2011; The Guardian for the text on p. 16 adapted from 'The Blind Marathon Runner who trains alone' by Mark Russell, *The Guardian* 16/04/2012, © Guardian News & Media Ltd 2012; The Guardian for the text on p. 19 adapted from comments following 'Teachers: we don't all want to go to uni', *The Guardian* 25/06/2012, © Guardian News & Media Ltd 2012; HarperCollins Publishers Ltd for text C on p. 30 adapted from *Tunnel vision, Journeys of an Underground Philosopher*, by Christopher Ross. Reprinted with permission of HarperCollins Publishers Ltd © 2002, Christopher Ross; Immediate Media Company Ltd for the text on p. 33 adapted from 'Pushed to Extremes' by Ed Chipperfield, published in *BBC In Knowledge Magazine*, © Immediate Media Company Ltd; National Geographic Creative for the text on p. 36, adapted from 'Scottish Island Obsession' by Jim Richardson, *National Geographic* 07/06/2011, © Jim Richardson/National Geographic Creative; Financial Times Limited for the text on p. 38 adapted from 'I'm in charge of the Hollywood sign' by Richard Pigden, *Financial Times Magazine* 15/08/2010, The Financial Times Limited 2010. All Rights Reserved; The Guardian for text A on p. 41 adapted from 'Sarah Storey: 'I have jam sandwiches passed to me when I'm cycling on the road' by Laura Wakelin, *The Guardian* 20/01/2012, © Guardian News & Media Ltd 2012; The Guardian for text B on p. 41 adapted from 'Jessica Ennis: 'I'm so hungry by the end of a heptathlon that I just want to indulge' by Laura Wakelin, *The Guardian* 20/01/2012, © Guardian News & Media Ltd 2012; The Guardian for text C on p. 41 adapted from 'Louis Smith: 'I make a good roast duck. I won Ready Steady Cook with it' by Laura Wakelin, *The Guardian* 20/01/2012, © Guardian News & Media Ltd 2012; The Guardian for text D on p. 41 adapted from Keri-Anne Payne: 'Swimming is my passion. Baking comes a close second' by Laura Wakelin, *The Guardian* 20/01/2012, © Guardian News & Media Ltd 2012; Nate Nault for the text on p. 47 adapted from '10 of my favorite study abroad photos and the story behind them', http://thestudyabroadblog. com/favorite-study-abroad-photos/; Copyright © by Nate Nault. Reprinted with permission; Yale University Press for the text on p. 54 adapted from *A Little Book of Language* by David Crystal, Yale University Press, © 2011; Hodder Paperbacks for the text on p. 58 adapted from *Nobbut A Lad. A Yorkshire Childhood* by Alan Titchmarsh. Reprinted with permission of Hodder Paperbacks, © 2007; The Guardian for the text on p. 60 adapted from 'Does music help you to run faster?' by Adharanand Finn, *The Guardian* 22/04/2012, © Guardian News & Media Ltd 2012; Immediate Media Company Ltd for text A p. 63 adapted from 'Horizon: Science for Everyone' by Tom Cole, published in *Radio Times* magazine 04/11/2008, © Immediate Media Company Ltd; Telegraph Media Group for text B on p. 63 adapted from 'Orbit: Earth's Extraordinary Journey, BBC Two, review' by Andrew Marsza, *The Telegraph* 05/03/2012, Copyright © Telegraph Media Group Limited, 2012; The Independent for text C on p. 63 adapted from 'The Weekend's TV: Wonders of the Universe, Sun, BBC2 Civilization: Is the West History? Reviewed by Tom Sutcliffe', by Tom Sutcliffe, *The Independent* 07/03/2011, Copyright © The Independent 2011; Immediate Media Company Ltd for text D on p. 63 adapted from 'Channel 4 to create a bionic human in groundbreaking science documentary' by Susanna Lazarus, published in *Radio Times* magazine 25/10/2012, © Immediate Media Company Ltd; Claire Morris for the text on p. 70 adapted from 'My Life as a Student Athlete', http://collegecandy. com/2010/07/30/my-life-as-a-student-athlete/; Copyright © by Claire Morris. Reprinted with permission; Quercus Publishing Plc for the text on p. 74 adapted from *Big Ideas in Brief* by Ian Crofton, Quercus Publishing Plc, © 2012. Reproduced with permission; John Lees for the text on p. 77 adapted from 'Personality stakes' by John Lees, *Metro*, Manchester 18/09/2012, © Metro; The Independent for the text on p. 77 adapted from 'How games have grown up to be a serious career aspiration' by Lauren Cope, *The Independent* 16/10/2012 © Copyright © The Independent 2012; Orion Books and World Famous Group for the text on p. 82 adapted from *Grand Prix Driver* by David Coulthard, © 2007, Orion Books and World Famous Group Ltd on behalf of David Coulthard with permission; The Guardian for text A on p. 85, adapted from 'Time Out not Time Off; Volunteering in Paradise by Teresa Machan, *The Guardian* 21/08/2010, © Guardian News & Media Ltd 2010; The Guardian for text B on p. 85 adapted from 'Eco holidays: Pass me that machete', *The Guardian* 19/09/2009, © Guardian News & Media Ltd 2009.

Photo acknowledgements

Key: T = Top, B = Below.

p. 38: Alamy/©Terry Harris; p. C1 (T): Getty Images/The Image Bank/Alistair Berg; p. C1 (B): Alamy/© Clynt Garnham Sport; p. C2 (T): Getty Images/The Image Bank/Peter Cade; p. C2 (B): Corbis/cultura/©Simon McComb; p. C4 (T): Getty Images/Photodisc/Andersen Ross; p. C4 (B): Getty ImagesE+/Nikki Bidgood; p. C5 (T): Corbis/©John Smith; p. C5 (B): Getty Images/Bloomberg/Chris Ratcliffe; p. C7 (T): Getty Images/Digital Vision/Briony Campbell; p. C7 (B): Getty Images/Flickr/Layland Masuda; p. C8 (T): Getty Images/Folio Images/ Lisa Bjorner; p. C8 (B): Getty Images/The Image Bank/Erik Von Weber; p. C10 (T): Getty Images/hemis.fr/Camille Moirenc; p. C10 (B): Alamy/©Kathy deWitt; p. C11 (T): Thinkstock/Purestock; p. C11 (B): Getty Images/Stone/Peter Dazeley.

The recordings which accompany this book were made at dsound, London.

Visual materials for the Speaking test

What do you think the people are enjoying about these football games?

1A

1B

What might be good or bad for the people about travelling in these ways?

1C

1D

1E

The best way to buy

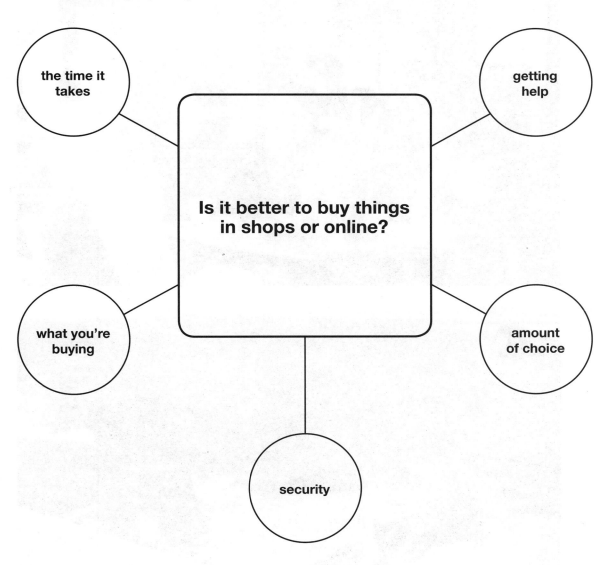

Why do you think the people are taking photographs in these situations?

2A

2B

What might be difficult for the people about doing these jobs?

2C

2D

2E

Television

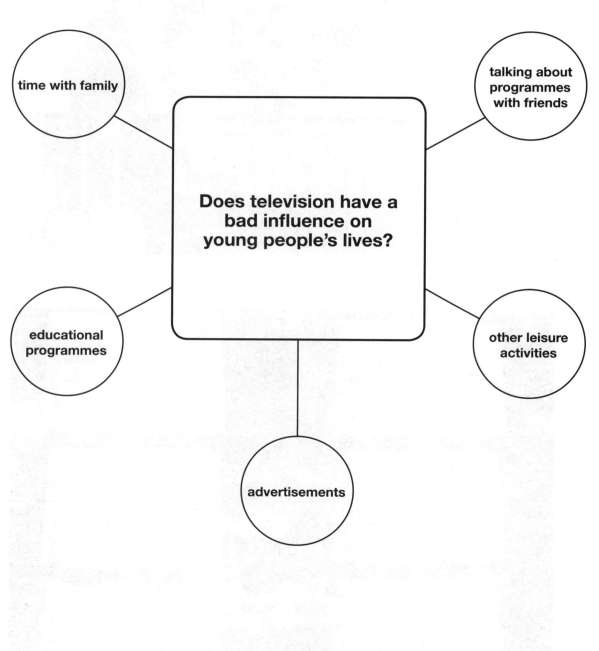

What are the people enjoying about doing these things in the evening?

3A

3B

Why have the families decided to do these things together in their free time?

3C

3D

3E

Television

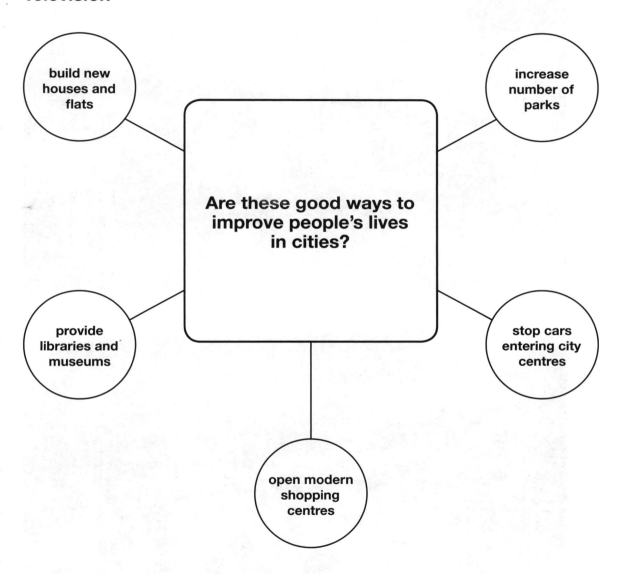

build new houses and flats

increase number of parks

Are these good ways to improve people's lives in cities?

provide libraries and museums

stop cars entering city centres

open modern shopping centres

Why have the people chosen to spend time in these different places in the city?

4A

4B

What might the people enjoy about their special day?

4C

4D

4E

Important things in life

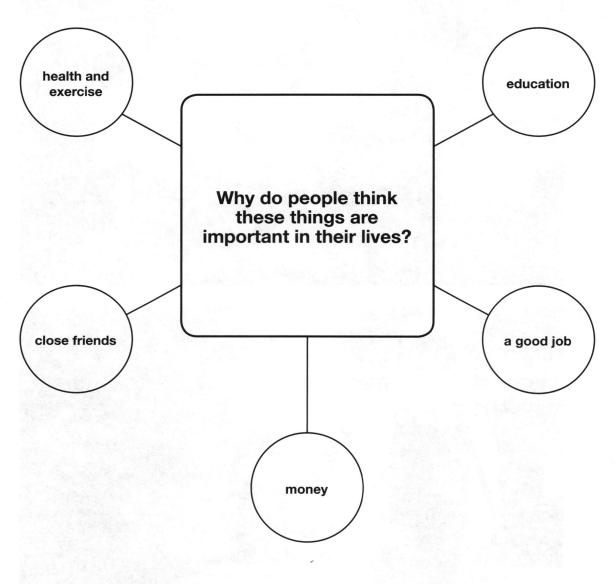

CARDIFF AND VALE COLLEGE